DEPARTMENT OF THE NAVY
HEADQUARTERS UNITED STATES MARINE CORPS
3000 MARINE CORPS PENTAGON
WASHINGTON, DC 20350-3000

I0415734

TRAIN THE TRAINER TRAINING AND READINESS MANUAL

NAVMC 3500.37A
C 469
4 May 09

NAVMC 3500.37A

From: Commandant of the Marine Corps
To: Distribution List

Subj: TRAIN THE TRAINER TRAINING AND READINESS MANUAL, (SHORT TITLE: T3 T&R MANUAL)

Ref: (a) MCO P3500.72A
       (b) MCO 1553.3A
       (c) MCO 3400.3F
       (d) MCO 3500.27B
       (e) MCRP 3-0A
       (f) MCRP 3-0B
       (g) MCO 1553.2A

1. Purpose. Training and educating Marines is the responsibility of the Commandant of the Marine Corps under US Code Title 10. Training and educating subordinates to carry out their duties and preparing them to carry out duties of the next grade is a common skill and inherent responsibility of all Marine Corps leaders regardless of occupation, billet or grade. In order to facilitate the accomplishment of these vitally important responsibilities there is an absolute requirement to train and educate the trainers who will train and educate Marines in our formal schools and those Marines who will conduct Unit Training Management (UTM) for all Marine units. Per reference (a), this T&R Manual establishes Core Capability Mission Essential Tasks (METS) to standardize training of Marine Corps formal school instructors, curriculum developers, and unit training managers. Additionally, it provides tasking for Train the Trainer School (T3) (formerly Instructional Management School (IMS)), preparing personnel for service in formal schools, PME schools, and training detachments, as well as unit training managers/leaders assigned to the operating forces and supporting establishment. This NAVMC supersedes MCO 1510.69C, Individual Training Standards for Formal School Faculty, and NAVMC 3500.37 dated 7 Feb 2008.

2. Scope

    a. The T3 School will use references (a) through (g) to ensure programs of instruction meet skill-training requirements established in this manual.

    b. The Core METS in this manual are specifically used to provide focus to the development of training standards for formal school instruction, curriculum development, and UTM. Reference (g) details the requirement for formal schools, PME schools, and training detachments to train formal school instructors and curriculum developers. Formal school readiness will be assessed via the Training and Education Command (TECOM) Commanding Generals Inspection Program (CGIP) utilizing the AIRS 400 inspection checklist. The

AIRS 400 checklist evaluates formal school/PME school/training detachment compliance with the requirement to train formal school instructors and curriculum developers, via T3 formal courses that utilize individual training events in this manual.

    c. Efficient and effective UTM is critical to the combat readiness of the Marine Corps. Reference (b) provides guidance to commanders in the conduct of internal assessment of the unit's ability to execute each assigned MET, and develop long-, mid-, and short-range training plans to sustain proficiency in each MET. Personnel assigned to billets involved in the UTM process will be trained in accordance with individual events for UTM contained in this manual. The T3 School will be the proponent for standardized UTM via Mobile Training Team training and will assist commanders in building training plans that make the best use of time and resources while sustaining MET proficiency and combat readiness.

3. <u>Information</u>. CG, TECOM will update this T&R Manual as necessary to provide current and relevant training standards to commanders. All questions pertaining to the Marine Corps Ground T&R Program and UTM should be directed to: Commanding General, TECOM (Ground Training Branch C 469), 1019 Elliot Road, Quantico, VA 22134.

4. <u>Command</u>. This Directive is applicable to the Marine Corps Total Force.

5. <u>Certification</u>. Reviewed and approved this date.

M. G. SPIESE
By direction

Distribution: PCN 10031974000

    Copy to: 7000260 (2)
              8145001 (1)

LOCATOR SHEET

Subj: TRAIN THE TRAINER TRAINING AND READINESS MANUAL, (SHORT TITLE: T3 T&R
       MANUAL)

Location: _____
                (Indicate location(s) of copy(ies) of this Manual.)

RECORD OF CHANGES

Log completed change action as indicated.

Change Number	Date of Change	Date Entered	Signature of Person Incorporated Change

T3 T&R MANUAL

TABLE OF CONTENTS

CHAPTER

1 . . . . OVERVIEW

2 . . . . MISSION ESSENTIAL TASKS MATRIX

3 . . . . FORMAL SCHOOL INSTRUCTOR INDIVIDUAL
EVENTS

4 . . . . FORMAL SCHOOL CURRICULUM DEVELOPER
                                      INDIVIDUAL EVENTS

5 . . . . FORMAL SCHOOL MANAGER INDIVIDUAL
                                      EVENTS

6 . . . . UNIT READINESS PLANNING INDIVIDUAL
                                      EVENTS

APPENDICES

A . . . . FUNCTIONAL AREA MATRIX

B . . . . TERMS AND DEFINITIONS

T3 T&R MANUAL

CHAPTER 1

OVERVIEW

	PARAGRAPH	PAGE
INTRODUCTION.	1000	1-2
UNIT TRAINING	1001	1-2
UNIT TRAINING MANAGEMENT.	1002	1-3
SUSTAINMENT AND EVALUATION OF TRAINING.	1003	1-3
T & R MANUAL ORGANIZATION	1004	1-4
T&R EVENT CODING.	1005	1-5
COMBAT READINESS PERCENTAGE.	1006	1-5
EVALUATION-CODED (E-CODED) EVENTS	1007	1-6
CRP CALCULATION	1008	1-6
T&R EVENT COMPOSITION	1009	1-7
CBRNE TRAINING.	1010	1-9
NIGHT TRAINING.	1011	1-10
OPERATIONAL RISK MANAGEMENT (ORM)	1012	1-10
APPLICATION OF SIMULATION	1013	1-11
MARINE CORPS GROUND T&R PROGRAM	1014	1-11

T3 T&R MANUAL

CHAPTER 1

OVERVIEW

1000. INTRODUCTION

1. The T&R Program is the Corps' primary tool for planning, conducting and evaluating training and assessing training readiness. Subject Matter Experts (SMEs) from the operating forces developed core capability Mission Essential Task Lists (METLs) for ground communities derived from the Marine Corps Task List (MCTL). T&R Manuals are built around these METLs and all events contained in T&R Manuals relate directly to this METL. This comprehensive T&R Program will help to ensure the Marine Corps continues to improve its combat readiness by training more efficiently and effectively. Ultimately, this will enhance the Marine Corps' ability to accomplish real-world missions.

2. The T&R Manual contains the individual and collective training requirements to prepare units to accomplish their combat mission. The T&R Manual is not intended to be an encyclopedia that contains every minute detail of how to accomplish training. Instead, it identifies the minimum standards that Marines must be able to perform. The T&R Manual is a fundamental tool for commanders to build and maintain unit combat readiness. Using this tool, leaders can construct and execute an effective training plan that supports the unit's METL. More detailed information on the Marine Corps Ground T&R Program is found in reference (a).

1001. UNIT TRAINING

1. The training of Marines to perform as an integrated unit in combat lies at the heart of the T&R program. Unit and individual readiness are directly related. Individual training and the mastery of individual core skills serve as the building blocks for unit combat readiness. A Marine's ability to perform critical skills required in combat is essential. However, it is not necessary to have all individuals within a unit fully trained in order for that organization to accomplish its assigned tasks. Manpower shortfalls, temporary assignments, leave, or other factors outside the commander's control, often affect the ability to conduct individual training. During these periods, unit readiness is enhanced if emphasis is placed on the individual training of Marines on-hand. Subsequently, these Marines will be mission ready and capable of executing as part of a team when the full complement of personnel is available.

2. Commanders will ensure that all tactical training is focused on their combat mission. The T&R Manual is a tool to help develop the unit's training plan. In most cases, unit training should focus on achieving unit proficiency in the core capabilities METL. However, commanders will adjust their training focus to support METLs associated with a major OPLAN/CONPLAN or named operation as designated by their higher commander and reported accordingly in the Defense Readiness Reporting System (DRRS). Tactical

training will support the METL in use by the commander and be tailored to
meet T&R standards. Commanders at all levels are responsible for effective
combat training. The conduct of training in a professional manner consistent
with Marine Corps standards cannot be over emphasized.

3. Commanders will provide personnel the opportunity to attend formal and
operational level courses of instruction as required by this Manual.
Attendance at all formal courses must enhance the warfighting capabilities of
the unit as determined by the unit commander.

1002. UNIT TRAINING MANAGEMENT

1. Unit Training Management (UTM) is the application of the Systems Approach
to Training and Education (SATE) and the Marine Corps Training Principles.
This is accomplished in a manner that maximizes training results and focuses
the training priorities of the unit in preparation for the conduct of its
wartime mission.

2. UTM techniques, described in references (b) and (e), provide commanders
with the requisite tools and techniques to analyze, design, develop,
implement, and evaluate the training of their unit. The Marine Corps
Training Principles, explained in reference (b), provide sound and proven
direction and are flexible enough to accommodate the demands of local
conditions. These principles are not inclusive, nor do they guarantee
success. They are guides that commanders can use to manage unit-training
programs. The Marine Corps training principles are:

    - Train as you fight
    - Make commanders responsible for training
    - Use standards-based training
    - Use performance-oriented training
    - Use mission-oriented training
    - Train the MAGTF to fight as a combined arms team
    - Train to sustain proficiency
    - Train to challenge

3. To maintain an efficient and effective training program, leaders at every
level must understand and implement UTM. Guidance for UTM and the process
for establishing effective programs are contained in references (a) through
(g).

1003. SUSTAINMENT AND EVALUATION OF TRAINING

1. The evaluation of training is necessary to properly prepare Marines for
combat. Evaluations are either formal or informal, and performed by members
of the unit (internal evaluation) or from an external command (external
evaluation).

2. Marines are expected to maintain proficiency in the training events for
their MOS at the appropriate grade or billet to which assigned. Leaders are
responsible for recording the training achievements of their Marines.
Whether it involves individual or collective training events, they must
ensure proficiency is sustained by requiring retraining of each event at or

before expiration of the designated sustainment interval. Performance of the training event, however, is not sufficient to ensure combat readiness. Leaders at all levels must evaluate the performance of their Marines and the unit as they complete training events, and only record successful accomplishment of training based upon the evaluation. The goal of evaluation is to ensure that correct methods are employed to achieve the desired standard, or the Marines understand how they need to improve in order to attain the standard. Leaders must determine whether credit for completing a training event is recorded if the standard was not achieved. While successful accomplishment is desired, debriefing of errors can result in successful learning that will allow ethical recording of training event completion. Evaluation is a continuous process that is integral to training management and is conducted by leaders at every level and during all phases of planning and the conduct of training. To ensure training is efficient and effective, evaluation is an integral part of the training plan. Ultimately, leaders remain responsible for determining if the training was effective.

3. The purpose of formal and informal evaluation is to provide commanders with a process to determine a unit's/Marine's proficiency in the tasks that must be performed in combat. Informal evaluations are conducted during every training evolution. Formal evaluations are often scenario-based, focused on the unit's METs, based on collective training standards, and usually conducted during higher-level collective events. References (a) and (f) provide further guidance on the conduct of informal and formal evaluations using the Marine Corps Ground T&R Program.

1004. T & R MANUAL ORGANIZATION

1. T&R Manuals are organized in one of two methods: unit-based or community-based. Unit-based T&R Manuals are written to support a type of unit (Infantry, Artillery, Tanks, etc.) and contain both collective and individual training standards. Community-based are written to support an Occupational Field, a group of related Military Occupational Specialties (MOSs), or billets within an organization (EOD, NBC, Intel, etc.), and usually only contain individual training standards. T&R Manuals are comprised of chapters that contain unit METs, collective training events (CTE), and individual training events (ITEs) for each MOS, billet, etc.

2. The T3 T&R Manual is a community-based manual comprised of 4 chapters. Because it is a community-based manual, not all the information contained in the Chapter 1 Overview is relevant to the application of the training standards in this manual. Chapter 1 amplifies general information contained in reference (a). Chapter 2 lists the Core Capability METs and their related Formal School Instructor, Curriculum Administrator, Formal School Manager, and Unit Training Management events. Chapters 3 and 4 contain individual events. The Train the Trainer School (formerly Instructional Management School (IMS)) will have proponency on Train the Trainer individual training standards.

1005. T&R EVENT CODING

1. T&R events are coded for ease of reference. Each event has up-to a 4-4-4-digit identifier. The first up-to four digits are referred to as a

"community" and represent the unit type or occupation (TANK, TOW, 1802, etc.). The second up-to four digits represent the functional or duty area (TAC, CMDC, GNRY, etc.). The last four digits represent the level and sequence of the event.

2. The T&R levels are illustrated in Figure 1. An example of the T&R coding is shown in Figure 2.

Figure 1: T&R Event Levels

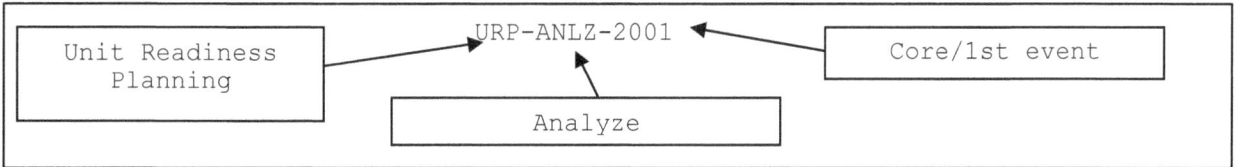

Figure 2: T&R Event Coding

1006. COMBAT READINESS PERCENTAGE

1. The Marine Corps Ground T&R Program includes processes to assess readiness of units and individual Marines. Every unit in the Marine Corps maintains a basic level of readiness based on the training and experience of the Marines in the unit. Even units that never trained together are capable of accomplishing some portion of their missions. Combat readiness assessment does not associate a quantitative value for this baseline of readiness, but uses a "Combat Readiness Percentage", as a method to provide a concise descriptor of the recent training accomplishments of units and Marines.

2. Combat Readiness Percentage (CRP) is the percentage of required training events that a unit or Marine accomplishes within specified sustainment intervals.

3. In unit-based T&R Manuals, unit combat readiness is assessed as a percentage of the successfully completed and current (within sustainment

interval) key training events called "Evaluation-Coded" (E-Coded) Events. E-Coded Events and unit CRP calculation are described in follow-on paragraphs. CRP achieved through the completion of E-Coded Events is directly relevant to readiness assessment in DRRS.

4. Individual combat readiness, in both unit-based and community-based T&R Manuals, is assessed as the percentage of required individual events in which a Marine is current. This translates as the percentage of training events for his/her MOS and grade (or billet) that the Marine successfully completes within the directed sustainment interval. Individual skills are developed through a combination of 1000-level training (entry-level formal school courses), individual on-the-job training in 2000-level events, and follow-on formal school training. Skill proficiency is maintained by retraining in each event per the specified sustainment interval.

1007. EVALUATION-CODED (E-CODED) EVENTS

1. Unit-type T&R Manuals can contain numerous unit events, some for the whole unit and others for integral parts that serve as building blocks for training. To simplify training management and readiness assessment, only collective events that are critical components of a mission essential task (MET), or key indicators of a unit's readiness, are used to generate CRP for a MET. These critical or key events are designated in the T&R Manual as Evaluation-Coded (E-Coded) events. Formal evaluation of unit performance in these events is recommended because of their value in assessing combat readiness. Only E-Coded events are used to calculate CRP for each MET.

2. The use of a METL-based training program allows the commander discretion in training. This makes the T&R Manual a training tool rather than a prescriptive checklist.

1008. CRP CALCULATION

1. Collective training begins at the 3000 level (team, crew or equivalent). Unit training plans are designed to accomplish the events that support the unit METL while simultaneously sustaining proficiency in individual core skills. Using the battalion-based (unit) model, the battalion (7000-level) has collective events that directly support a MET on the METL. These collective events are E-Coded and the only events that contribute to unit CRP. This is done to assist commanders in prioritizing the training toward the METL, taking into account resource, time, and personnel constraints.

2. Unit CRP increases after the completion of E-Coded events. The number of E-Coded events for the MET determines the value of each E-Coded event. For example, if there are 4 E-Coded events for a MET, each is worth 25% of MET CRP. MET CRP is calculated by adding the percentage of each completed and current (within sustainment interval) E-Coded training event. The percentage for each MET is calculated the same way and all are added together and divided by the number of METS to determine unit CRP. For ease of calculation, we will say that each MET has 4 E-Coded events, each contributing 25% towards the completion of the MET. If the unit has completed and is current on three of the four E-Coded events for a given MET, then they have completed 75% of the MET. The CRP for each MET is added

together and divided by the number of METS to get unit CRP; unit CRP is the average of MET CRP.

For Example:

    MET 1: 75% complete (3 of 4 E-Coded events trained)
    MET 2: 100% complete (6 of 6 E-Coded events trained)
    MET 3: 25% complete (1 of 4 E-Coded events trained)
    MET 4: 50% complete (2 of 4 E-Coded events trained)
    MET 5: 75% complete (3 of 4 E-Coded events trained)

To get unit CRP, simply add the CRP for each MET and divide by the number of METS:

    MET CRP: 75 + 100 + 25 + 50 + 75 = 325

    Unit CRP: 325 (total MET CRP)/ 5 (total number of METS) = 65%

1009. T&R EVENT COMPOSITION

1. This section explains each of the components of a T&R event. These items are included in all events in each T&R manual.

    a. Event Code (see Sect 1005). The event code is a 4-4-4 character set. For individual training events, the first 4 characters indicate the occupational function. The second 4 characters indicate functional area (TAC, CBTS, VOPS, etc.). The third 4 characters are simply a numerical designator for the event.

    b. Event Title. The event title is the name of the event.

    c. E-Coded. This is a "yes/no" category to indicate whether or not the event is E-Coded. If yes, the event contributes toward the CRP of the associated MET. The value of each E-Coded event is based on number of E-Coded events for that MET. Refer to paragraph 1008 for detailed explanation of E-Coded events.

    d. Supported MET(s). List all METs that are supported by the training event.

    e. Sustainment Interval. This is the period, expressed in number of months, between evaluation or retraining requirements. Skills and capabilities acquired through the accomplishment of training events are refreshed at pre-determined intervals. It is essential that these intervals are adhered to in order to ensure Marines maintain proficiency.

    f. Billet. Individual training events may contain a list of billets within the community that are responsible for performing that event. This ensures that the billets expected tasks are clearly articulated and a Marine's readiness to perform in that billet is measured.

    g. Grade. Each individual training event will list the rank(s) at which Marines are required to learn and sustain the training event.

h. <u>Initial Training Setting</u>. For Individual T&R Events only, this specifies the location for initial instruction of the training event in one of three categories (formal school, managed on-the-job training, distance learning). Regardless of the specified Initial Training Setting, any T&R event may be introduced and evaluated during managed on-the-job training.

(1) "FORMAL" – When the Initial Training Setting of an event is identified as "FORMAL" (formal school), the appropriate formal school or training detachment is required to provide initial training in the event. Conversely, formal schools and training detachments are not authorized to provide training in events designated as Initial Training Setting "MOJT" or "DL." Since the duration of formal school training must be constrained to optimize Operating Forces' manning, this element provides the mechanism for Operating Forces' prioritization of training requirements for both entry-level (1000-level) and career-level (2000-level) T&R Events. For formal schools and training detachments, this element defines the requirements for content of courses.

(2) "DL" – Identifies the training event as a candidate for initial training via a Distance Learning product (correspondence course or MarineNet course).

(3) "MOJT" – Events specified for Managed On-the-Job Training are to be introduced to Marines, and evaluated, as part of training within a unit by supervisory personnel.

i. <u>Event Description</u>. Provide a description of the event purpose, objectives, goals, and requirements. It is a general description of an action requiring learned skills and knowledge (e.g. Camouflage the M1A1 Tank).

j. <u>Condition</u>. Describe the condition(s), under which tasks are performed. Conditions are based on a "real world" operational environment. They indicate what is provided (equipment, materials, manuals, aids, etc.), environmental constraints, conditions under which the task is performed, and any specific cues or indicators to which the performer must respond. When resources or safety requirements limit the conditions, this is stated.

k. <u>Standard</u>. The standard indicates the basis for judging effectiveness of the performance. It consists of a carefully worded statement that identifies the proficiency level expected when the task is performed. The standard provides the minimum acceptable performance parameters and is strictly adhered to. The standard for collective events is general, describing the desired end-state or purpose of the event. While the standard for individual events specifically describe to what proficiency level in terms of accuracy, speed, sequencing, quality of performance, adherence to procedural guidelines, etc., the event is accomplished.

l. <u>Event Components</u>. Describe the actions composing the event and help the user determine what must be accomplished and to properly plan for the event.

m. <u>Prerequisite Events</u>. Prerequisites are academic training or other T&R events that must be completed prior to attempting the task. They are lower-level events or tasks that give the individual/unit the skills required to accomplish the event. They can also be planning steps, administrative requirements, or specific parameters that build toward mission accomplishment.

n. Chained Events. Collective T&R events are supported by lower-level collective and individual T&R events. This enables unit leaders to effectively identify subordinate T&R events that ultimately support specific mission essential tasks. When the accomplishment of any upper-level events, by their nature, result in the performance of certain subordinate and related events, the events are "chained." The completion of chained events will update sustainment interval credit (and CRP for E-Coded events) for the related subordinate level events.

o. Related Events. Provide a list of all Individual Training Standards that support the event.

p. References. The training references are utilized to determine task performance steps, grading criteria, and ensure standardization of training procedures. They assist the trainee in satisfying the performance standards, or the trainer in evaluating the effectiveness of task completion. References are also important to the development of detailed training plans.

q. Distance Learning Products (IMI, CBT, MCI, etc.). Include this component when the event can be taught via one of these media methods vice attending a formal course of instruction or receiving MOJT.

r. Support Requirements. This is a list of the external and internal support the unit and Marines will need to complete the event. The list includes, but is not limited to:

- Range(s)/Training Area
- Ordnance
- Equipment
- Materials
- Other Units/Personnel
- Other Support Requirements

s. Miscellaneous. Provide any additional information that assists in the planning and execution of the event. Miscellaneous information may include, but is not limited to:

- Admin Instructions
- Special Personnel Certifications
- Equipment Operating Hours
- Road Miles

2. Community-based T&R manuals may have several additional components not found in unit-based T&R manuals.

1010. CBRNE TRAINING

1. All personnel assigned to the operating force must be trained in chemical, biological, radiological, nuclear, and explosive incident defense (CBRNE), in order to survive and continue their mission in this environment.

Individual proficiency standards are defined as survival and basic operating standards. Survival standards are those that the individual must master in order to survive CBRNE attacks. Basic operating standards are those that the individual, and collectively the unit, must perform to continue operations in a CBRNE environment.

2. In order to develop and maintain the ability to operate in an CBRNE environment, CBRNE training is an integral part of the training plan and events in this T&R Manual. Units should train under CBRNE conditions whenever possible. Per reference (c), all units must be capable of accomplishing their assigned mission in a contaminated environment.

1011. NIGHT TRAINING

1. While it is understood that all personnel and units of the operating force are capable of performing their assigned mission in "every climate and place," current doctrine emphasizes the requirement to perform assigned missions at night and during periods of limited visibility. Basic skills are significantly more difficult when visibility is limited.

2. To ensure units are capable of accomplishing their mission they must train under the conditions of limited visibility. Units should strive to conduct all events in this T&R Manual during both day and night/limited visibility conditions. When there is limited training time available, night training should take precedence over daylight training, contingent on individual, crew, and unit proficiency.

1012. OPERATIONAL RISK MANAGEMENT (ORM)

1. ORM is a process that enables commanders to plan for and minimize risk while still accomplishing the mission. It is a decision making tool used by Marines at all levels to increase operational effectiveness by anticipating hazards and reducing the potential for loss, thereby increasing the probability of a successful mission. ORM minimizes risks to acceptable levels, commensurate with mission accomplishment.

2. Commanders, leaders, maintainers, planners, and schedulers will integrate risk assessment in the decision-making process and implement hazard controls to reduce risk to acceptable levels. Applying the ORM process will reduce mishaps, lower costs, and provide for more efficient use of resources. ORM assists the commander in conserving lives and resources and avoiding unnecessary risk, making an informed decision to implement a course of action (COA), identifying feasible and effective control measures where specific measures do not exist, and providing reasonable alternatives for mission accomplishment. Most importantly, ORM assists the commander in determining the balance between training realism and unnecessary risks in training, the impact of training operations on the environment, and the adjustment of training plans to fit the level of proficiency and experience of Sailors/Marines and leaders. Further guidance for ORM is found in references (b) and (d).

1013. APPLICATION OF SIMULATION

1. Simulations/Simulators and other training devices shall be used when they are capable of effectively and economically supplementing training on the identified training task. Particular emphasis shall be placed on simulators that provide training that might be limited by safety considerations or constraints on training space, time, or other resources. When deciding on simulation issues, the primary consideration shall be improving the quality of training and consequently the state of readiness. Potential savings in operating and support costs normally shall be an important secondary consideration.

2. Each training event contains information relating to the applicability of simulation. If simulator training applies to the event, then the applicable simulator(s) is/are listed in the "Simulation" section and the CRP for simulation training is given. This simulation training can either be used in place of live training, at the reduced CRP indicated; or can be used as a precursor training for the live event, i.e., weapons simulators, convoy trainers, observed fire trainers, etc. It is recommended that tasks be performed by simulation prior to being performed in a live-fire environment. However, in the case where simulation is used as a precursor for the live event, then the unit will receive credit for the live event CRP only. If a tactical situation develops that precludes performing the live event, the unit would then receive credit for the simulation CRP.

1014. MARINE CORPS GROUND T&R PROGRAM

1. The Marine Corps Ground T&R Program continues to evolve. The vision for Ground T&R Program is to publish a T&R Manual for every readiness-reporting unit so that core capability METs are clearly defined with supporting collective training standards, and to publish community-based T&R Manuals for all occupational fields whose personnel augment other units to increase their combat and/or logistic capabilities. The vision for this program includes plans to provide a Marine Corps training management information system that enables tracking of unit and individual training accomplishments by unit commanders and small unit leaders, automatically computing CRP for both units and individual Marines based upon MOS and rank (or billet). Linkage of T&R Events to the Marine Corps Task List (MCTL), through the core capability METs, has enabled objective assessment of training readiness in the DRRS.

2. DRRS measures and reports on the readiness of military forces and the supporting infrastructure to meet missions and goals assigned by the Secretary of Defense. With unit CRP based on the unit's training toward its METs, the CRP will provide a more accurate picture of a unit's readiness. This will give fidelity to future funding requests and factor into the allocation of resources. Additionally, the Ground T&R Program will help to ensure training remains focused on mission accomplishment and that training readiness reporting is tied to units' METLs.

T3 T&R MANUAL

CHAPTER 2

MISSION ESSENTIAL TASKS MATRIX

	PARAGRAPH	PAGE
T3 MISSION ESSENTIAL TASKS MATRIX	2000	2-2

CHAPTER 2

MISSION ESSENTIAL TASKS MATRIX

2000. T3 MISSION ESSENTIAL TASKS MATRIX. The T3 Mission Essential Task List (METL) Table includes the designated MET number. There are no E-coded events in the T3 T&R Manual. This matrix reflects all events and the MET they support.

MET#/MISSION ESSENTIAL TASK

MET 1. Implement Formal School Instruction	
FSIC-IMPI-2101	Prepare for instruction
FSIC-IMPI-2102	Employ Instructional Communication
FSIC-IMPI-2103	Conduct a Lesson
FSIC-IMPI-2104	Conduct After Lesson Management
AIC-IMPL-2201	Recommend Changes to Instructional Materials
AIC-IMPL-2202	Employ Advanced Instructional Methods
AIC-IMPL-2203	Develop Instructors
AIC-IMPL-2204	Motivate Students
AIC-IMPL-2205	Employ Advanced Facilitation Techniques
MET 2. Develop Formal School Curricula	
CDC-DESI-2013	Write a Target Population Description
CDC-DESI-2014	Conduct a Learning Analysis
CDC-DESI-2015	Develop Learning Objectives
CDC-DESI-2016	Select Instructional Methods
CDC-DESI-2017	Select Instructional Media
CDC-DESI-2018	Write Test Items
CDC-DESI-2019	Sequence Terminal Learning Objectives
CDC-DEVI-2012	Assemble a Master Lesson File
CDC-DEVI-2020	Develop a Course Structure
CDC-DEVI-2021	Develop Concept Cards
CDC-DEVI-2022	Develop a Program of Instruction
CDC-DEVI-2023	Construct a Test
CDC-DEVI-2024	Conduct Validation
CDC-DEVI-2025	Conduct an In-Depth Operational Risk Assessment
CDC-DEVI-2026	Write an Instructor Preparation Guide
CDC-DEVI-2027	Write a Lesson Plan
CDC-DEVI-2028	Write Student Materials
CDC-DEVI-2029	Develop Instructional Media
CDC-TIMS-2011	Use Automated System in Curriculum Development

MET 3. Conduct Formal School Management

FSM-ANLZ-2001	Develop a T&R Event
FSM-DESI-2006	Integrate Adult Learning Theory into Curriculum Development
FSM-EVLI-2007	Implement a Formal School Evaluation Plan
FSM-EVLI-2008	Assist in a Course Content Review Board
FSM-MANI-2002	Implement a Formal School Academic Standard Operating Procedure
FSM-MANI-2003	Implement a Staff and Faculty Development Plan
FSM-MANI-2004	Develop a Memorandum of Agreement/Understanding
FSM-MANI-2005	Conduct Operational Risk Assessment
FSM-TIMS-2009	Administrate the Use of MCTIMS

MET 4. Instruct Unit Readiness Planning (URP)

URP-ANLZ-2001	Develop a METL
URP-DESI-2006	Conduct Training Assessment
URP-DESI-2007	Determine Training Strategy
URP-DESI-2008	Develop Training Guidance
URP-DESI-2009	Develop a Long Range Training Plan
URP-DESI-2010	Develop a Mid Range Training Plan
URP-DESI-2011	Develop a Short Range Training Plan
URP-DESI-2012	Develop Training Schedules
URP-DEVI-2016	Conduct Unit Training
URP-DEVI-2017	Prepare for Training
URP-DEVI-2019	Conduct Operational Risk Assessment
URP-EVLI-2015	Conduct After-Action Review
URP-EVLI-2028	Evaluate Training
URP-IMPI-2024	Conduct Training

T3 T&R MANUAL

CHAPTER 3

FORMAL SCHOOL INSTRUCTION INDIVIDUAL EVENTS

	PARAGRAPH	PAGE
PURPOSE	3000	3-2
ADMINISTRATIVE NOTES	3001	3-2
INDEX OF INDIVIDUAL EVENTS	3002	3-3
2000-LEVEL EVENTS	3003	3-4

T3 T&R MANUAL

CHAPTER 3

FORMAL SCHOOL INSTRUCTION INDIVIDUAL EVENTS

3000. PURPOSE. This chapter details the individual events that pertain to formal school instruction. These events are linked to a Mission Essential Task (MET) developed to guide T3 community training. This linkage tailor's individual training for the selected MET. Each individual event provides an event title, along with the conditions events will be performed under, and the standard to which the event must be performed to be successful.

3001. ADMINISTRATIVE NOTES. T&R events are coded for ease of reference. Each event has a 4-4-4 digit identifier. The first four digits represent the occupational field or military occupational field (FSIC, AIC, OR URP). The second four digits represent the functional or duty area (ANLZ, DESI, etc.). The last four digits represent the level, and identifier number of the event. Every individual event has an identifier number from 001 to 999.

3002. INDEX OF INDIVIDUAL EVENTS

EVENT	TITLE	PAGE
	2000 LEVEL EVENTS	
FSIC-IMPI-2101	Prepare for Instruction	3-4
FSIC-IMPI-2102	Employ Instructional Communication	3-4
FSIC-IMPI-2103	Conduct a Lesson	3-5
FSIC-IMPI-2104	Conduct After Lesson Management	3-5
AIC-IMPL-2201	Recommend Changes to Instructional Materials	3-6
AIC-IMPL-2202	Employ Advanced Instructional Methods	3-6
AIC-IMPL-2203	Develop Instructors	3-7
AIC-IMPL-2204	Motivate Students	3-7
AIC-IMPL-2205	Employ Advanced Facilitation Techniques	3-8

3003. 2000-LEVEL EVENTS

FSIC-IMPI-2101: Prepare for Instruction

EVALUATION-CODED: NO   **SUSTAINMENT INTERVAL:** 3 months

GRADES: CPL, SGT, SSGT, GYSGT, MSGT, MGYSGT, WO-1, CWO-2, CWO-3, CWO-4, CWO-5, 2NDLT, 1STLT, CAPT, MAJ, LTCOL

INITIAL TRAINING SETTING: FORMAL

CONDITION: Given a Master Lesson File, an instructional setting, and references.

STANDARD: In accordance with the Systems Approach to Training (SAT) Manual chapter 4 sections 4100 and 4300.

PERFORMANCE STEPS:
1. Review course/training schedule
2. Review lesson materials
3. Assess time critical risk factors
4. Prepare instructional environment
5. Conduct rehearsals

REFERENCES:
1. SAT MANUAL Systems Approach to Training Manual

FSIC-IMPI-2102: Employ Instructional Communication

EVALUATION-CODED: YES   **SUSTAINMENT INTERVAL:** 3 months

GRADES: CPL, SGT, SSGT, GYSGT, MSGT, MGYSGT, WO-1, CWO-2, CWO-3, CWO-4, CWO-5, 2NDLT, 1STLT, CAPT, MAJ, LTCOL

INITIAL TRAINING SETTING: FORMAL

CONDITION: Given a Master Lesson File, an instructional setting, and references.

STANDARD: In accordance with the Systems Approach to Training (SAT) Manual chapter 4 section 4400.

PERFORMANCE STEPS:
1. Employ verbal communication techniques
2. Employ non-verbal communication techniques
3. Employ listening techniques
4. Employ questioning techniques
5. Employ facilitation techniques

REFERENCES:
1. SAT MANUAL Systems Approach to Training Manual

FSIC-IMPI-2103: Conduct a Lesson

EVALUATION-CODED: NO   **SUSTAINMENT INTERVAL**: 3 months

GRADES: CPL, SGT, SSGT, GYSGT, MSGT, MGYSGT, WO-1, CWO-2, CWO-3, CWO-4, CWO-5, 2NDLT, 1STLT, CAPT, MAJ, LTCOL

INITIAL TRAINING SETTING: FORMAL

CONDITION: Given a Master Lesson File, an instructional setting, and references.

STANDARD: In accordance with the Systems Approach to Training (SAT) Manual chapter 4 section 4400.

PERFORMANCE STEPS:
1. Introduce a lesson
2. Present the main body of the lesson
3. Present instructional methods
4. Employ media
5. Summarize the lesson

REFERENCES:
1. SAT MANUAL Systems Approach to Training Manual

FSIC-IMPI-2104: Conduct After Lesson Management

EVALUATION-CODED: NO   **SUSTAINMENT INTERVAL**: 3 months

GRADES: CPL, SGT, SSGT, GYSGT, MSGT, MGYSGT, WO-1, CWO-2, CWO-3, CWO-4, CWO-5, 2NDLT, 1STLT, CAPT, MAJ, LTCOL

INITIAL TRAINING SETTING: FORMAL

CONDITION: After the completion of a lesson given evaluation forms, and references.

STANDARD: In accordance with the Systems Approach to Training (SAT) Manual chapter 4 section 4600.

PERFORMANCE STEPS:
1. Remove media
2. Secure classified materials
3. Reset the instructional environment
4. Conduct clean up
5. Turn-in any borrowed equipment and resources
6. Review school SOP for additional after lesson actions
7. Collect data
8. Analyze data
9. Record time critical operational risk assessment effectiveness
10. Complete after instruction reports

REFERENCES:
1. SAT MANUAL Systems Approach to Training Manual

AIC-IMPL-2201: Recommend Changes to Instructional Materials

EVALUATION-CODED: NO   **SUSTAINMENT INTERVAL:** 12 months

GRADES: SGT, SSGT, GYSGT, MSGT, MGYSGT, WO-1, CWO-2, CWO-3, CWO-4, CWO-5, 2NDLT, 1STLT, CAPT, MAJ, LTCOL, COL

INITIAL TRAINING SETTING: FORMAL

CONDITION: Given instructional materials and references.

STANDARD: To ensure instructional materials are complete and current in accordance with the Systems Approach to Training (SAT) Manual chapter 3 section 3800.

PERFORMANCE STEPS:
1. Recommend changes to the learning analysis work sheet
2. Recommend changes to the learning objective work sheet
3. Recommend changes to the concept card
4. Recommend changes to the operational risk assessment sheet
5. Recommend changes to the instructor preparation guide
6. Recommend changes to the lesson plan
7. Recommend changes to the student outline
8. Recommend changes to the student supplemental material
9. Recommend changes to media
10. Recommend changes to the training schedule

REFERENCES:
1. SAT MANUAL Systems Approach to Training Manual

AIC-IMPL-2202: Employ Advanced Instructional Methods

EVALUATION-CODED: NO   **SUSTAINMENT INTERVAL:** 3 months

GRADES: SGT, SSGT, GYSGT, MSGT, MGYSGT, WO-1, CWO-2, CWO-3, CWO-4, CWO-5, 2NDLT, 1STLT, CAPT, MAJ, LTCOL, COL

INITIAL TRAINING SETTING: FORMAL

CONDITION: Given instructional materials and references.

STANDARD: To ensure the transfer of knowledge and skills.

PERFORMANCE STEPS:
1. Employ Guided Discussions
2. Employ Peer Teaching Exercises
3. Employ a Case Study
4. Employ Gaming Techniques
5. Employ Mentoring Techniques
6. Employ Role Playing Techniques

7. Employ Tactical Decision Games
8. Employ Apprenticeship techniques
9. Employ Sand Table Exercises

REFERENCES:
1. Air Force Manual 36-2236 (Nov 2003) GUIDEBOOK FOR AIR FORCE INSTRUCTORS

MISCELLANEOUS:

    ADMINISTRATIVE INSTRUCTIONS: Instructional Materials may include: Facilitation guides for advanced methods and any/all components of the MLF

AIC-IMPL-2203: Develop Instructors

EVALUATION-CODED: NO   **SUSTAINMENT INTERVAL:** 12 months

GRADES: SGT, SSGT, GYSGT, MSGT, MGYSGT, WO-1, CWO-2, CWO-3, CWO-4, CWO-5, 2NDLT, 1STLT, CAPT, MAJ, LTCOL, COL

INITIAL TRAINING SETTING: FORMAL

CONDITION: Given a staff and faculty development plan, instructors, and references.

STANDARD: To ensure instructors are certified in all classes they are required to teach; and in accordance with the Systems Approach to Training (SAT) Manual chapter 7, section 7202.

PERFORMANCE STEPS:
1. Implement the Staff & Faculty Development Plan
2. Provide Instructor Orientation
3. Mentor Instructors
4. Train Instructors
5. Evaluate Instructors
6. Record Individual Instructor Training

REFERENCES:
1. Air Force Manual 36-2236 (Nov 2003) GUIDEBOOK FOR AIR FORCE INSTRUCTORS
2. SAT MANUAL Systems Approach to Training Manual

AIC-IMPL-2204: Motivate Students

EVALUATION-CODED: NO   **SUSTAINMENT INTERVAL:** 3 months

GRADES: SGT, SSGT, GYSGT, MSGT, MGYSGT, WO-1, CWO-2, CWO-3, CWO-4, CWO-5, 2NDLT, 1STLT, CAPT, MAJ, LTCOL, COL

INITIAL TRAINING SETTING: FORMAL

CONDITION: Given a lesson to instruct, an instructional setting, and references.

STANDARD: To generate and enhance interest in the subject matter.

PERFORMANCE STEPS:
1. Apply Motivation theory
2. Apply the Hierarchy of Motivation
3. Apply Motivation Principles

REFERENCES:
1. Enhancing Adult Motivation to Learn A Comprehensive Guide for Teaching All Adults Raymond J. Wlodkowski

---

AIC-IMPL-2205: Employ Advanced Facilitation Techniques

EVALUATION-CODED: NO   **SUSTAINMENT INTERVAL:** 3 months

GRADES: SGT, SSGT, GYSGT, MSGT, MGYSGT, WO-1, CWO-2, CWO-3, CWO-4, CWO-5, 2NDLT, 1STLT, CAPT, MAJ, LTCOL, COL

INITIAL TRAINING SETTING: FORMAL

CONDITION: Given a lesson to facilitate, instructional materials, instructional setting, and references.

STANDARD: To enhance student learning to achieve the learning objectives.

PERFORMANCE STEPS:
1. Relate as a Story Teller
2. Employ Opening Techniques
3. Increase Responsibility for Learning
4. Employ Training Tools
5. Refocus Students
6. Draw Partial Mind Mapping
7. Manage Difficult Students
8. Employ Closing Techniques
9. Connect to previous learning
10. Guide participation
11. Encourage peer interaction

REFERENCES:
1. Influencer The Power to Change Anything: Grenny, Maxfield, McMillan, Patterson, Switzler

---

T3 T&R MANUAL

CHAPTER 4

FORMAL SCHOOL CURRICULUM DEVELOPER INDIVIDUAL EVENTS

	PARAGRAPH	PAGE
PURPOSE	4000	4-2
ADMINISTRATIVE NOTES.	4001	4-2
INDEX OF INDIVIDUAL EVENTS.	4002	4-3
2000-LEVEL EVENTS	4003	4-4

T3 T&R MANUAL

CHAPTER 4

FORMAL SCHOOL CURRICULUM DEVELOPER INDIVIDUAL EVENTS

4000. PURPOSE. This chapter details the individual events that pertain to the T3 community. These events are linked to designated formal school Mission Essential Tasks (MET). This linkage tailor's individual training for the selected MET. Each individual event provides an event title, along with the conditions events will be performed under, and the standard to which the event must be performed to be successful.

4001. ADMINISTRATIVE NOTES. T&R events are coded for ease of reference. Each event has a 4-4-4 digit identifier. The first four digits represent the occupational field or military occupational field (URP, or FSIC). The second four digits represent the functional or duty area (ANLZ, DESI, etc.). The last four digits represent the level, and identifier number of the event. Every individual event has an identifier number from 001 to 999.

4002. INDEX OF INDIVIDUAL EVENTS

EVENT	TITLE	PAGE
	2000 LEVEL EVENTS	
CDC-DESI-2013	Write a Target Population Description	4-4
CDC-DESI-2014	Conduct a Learning Analysis	4-4
CDC-DESI-2015	Develop Learning Objectives	4-5
CDC-DESI-2016	Select Instructional Methods	4-5
CDC-DESI-2017	Select Instructional Media	4-6
CDC-DESI-2018	Write Test Items	4-6
CDC-DESI-2019	Sequence Terminal Learning Objectives	4-7
CDC-DEVI-2012	Assemble a Master Lesson File	4-7
CDC-DEVI-2020	Develop a Course Structure	4-8
CDC-DEVI-2021	Develop Concept Cards	4-8
CDC-DEVI-2022	Develop a Program of Instruction	4-9
CDC-DEVI-2023	Construct a Test	4-10
CDC-DEVI-2024	Conduct Validation	4-10
CDC-DEVI-2025	Conduct an In-Depth Operational Risk Assessment	4-11
CDC-DEVI-2026	Write an Instructor Preparation Guide	4-11
CDC-DEVI-2027	Write a Lesson Plan	4-12
CDC-DEVI-2028	Write Student Materials	4-12
CDC-DEVI-2029	Develop Instructional Media	4-13
CDC-TIMS-2011	Use the Automated System in Curriculum Development	4-13

4003. 2000-LEVEL EVENTS

CDC-DESI-2013: Write a Target Population Description

EVALUATION-CODED: NO   **SUSTAINMENT INTERVAL**: 24 months

GRADES: SGT, SSGT, GYSGT, MSGT, MGYSGT, WO-1, CWO-2, CWO-3, CWO-4, CWO-5, 2NDLT, 1STLT, CAPT, MAJ, LTCOL, COL

INITIAL TRAINING SETTING: FORMAL

CONDITION: Given the required instructional materials and equipment and with the aid of references.

STANDARD: That describes the administrative, physical, and academic characteristics of the average student attending the course in accordance with the Systems Approach to Training (SAT) Manual chapter 2, section 2100.

PERFORMANCE STEPS:
1. Obtain sources of data.
2. Review sources of data.
3. Organize data into categories.
4. Record the Target Population Description (TPD).

REFERENCES:
1. MCTIMS USER MANUAL
2. SAT MANUAL Systems Approach to Training Manual

CDC-DESI-2014: Conduct a Learning Analysis

EVALUATION-CODED: NO   **SUSTAINMENT INTERVAL**: 24 months

GRADES: SGT, SSGT, GYSGT, MSGT, MGYSGT, WO-1, CWO-2, CWO-3, CWO-4, CWO-5, 2NDLT, 1STLT, CAPT, MAJ, LTCOL, COL

INITIAL TRAINING SETTING: FORMAL

CONDITION: Given the necessary materials and equipment and with the aid of references.

STANDARD: That defines what will be taught by generating sequenced groups of Knowledge Skills and Attitudes in accordance with the Systems Approach to Training (SAT) Manual chapter 2 section 2200.

PERFORMANCE STEPS:
1. Gather materials.
2. Determine training requirements.
3. Analyze the Target Population Description (TPD).
4. Record task/event data on the Learning Analysis Worksheet (LAW).
5. Generate Knowledge, Skills, and Attitudes (KSAs) for each performance step.
6. Group Knowledge, Skills, and Attitudes (KSAs) into common areas.

7. Sequence groupings.
8. Record Learning Analysis in MCTIMS.

REFERENCES:
1. MCTIMS USER MANUAL
2. SAT MANUAL Systems Approach to Training Manual

CDC-DESI-2015: Develop Learning Objectives

EVALUATION-CODED: NO   **SUSTAINMENT INTERVAL:** 24 months

GRADES: SGT, SSGT, GYSGT, MSGT, MGYSGT, WO-1, CWO-2, CWO-3, CWO-4, CWO-5, 2NDLT, 1STLT, CAPT, MAJ, LTCOL, COL

INITIAL TRAINING SETTING: FORMAL

CONDITION: Given completed Learning Analysis Worksheets, materials and equipment, and with the aid of references.

STANDARD: That describe the behavior, condition, and standard consistent with the domain and level of learning in accordance with the Systems Approach to Training (SAT) Manual chapter 2 section 2202 and the SAT manual chapter 6.

PERFORMANCE STEPS:
1. Record behavior from T&R Manual for the Terminal Learning Objective (TLO).
2. Record condition from T&R Manual for the Terminal Learning Objective (TLO).
3. Record standard from T&R Manual for the Terminal Learning Objective (TLO).
4. Compare formal school resources to task behavior.
5. Determine evaluation methods.
6. Complete the Terminal Learning Objective (TLO) on Learning Objective Worksheet (LOW).
7. Document the behavior from grouped KSAs for Enabling Learning Objective (ELO).
8. Determine the condition for Enabling Learning Objective (ELO).
9. Determine the standard for Enabling Learning Objective (ELO).
10. Complete Enabling Learning Objective (ELO) on Learning Objective Worksheet (LOW).

REFERENCES:
1. MCTIMS USER MANUAL
2. SAT MANUAL Systems Approach to Training Manual

CDC-DESI-2016: Select Instructional Methods

EVALUATION-CODED: NO   **SUSTAINMENT INTERVAL:** 24 months

GRADES: SGT, SSGT, GYSGT, 1STSGT, MSGT, SGTMAJ, MGYSGT, WO-1, CWO-2, CWO-3, CWO-4, CWO-5, 2NDLT, 1STLT, CAPT, MAJ, LTCOL, COL

INITIAL TRAINING SETTING: FORMAL

CONDITION: Given Learning Objectives, Target Population Description, necessary materials and equipment, and with the aid of references.

STANDARD: Consistent with the domain and level of learning within the learning objective behaviors in accordance with the Systems Approach to Training (SAT) Manual chapter 2 section 2208 and the SAT Manual chapter 6.

PERFORMANCE STEPS:
1. Review method considerations.
2. Record instructional method(s) on the Learning Objective Worksheet (LOW).

REFERENCES:
1. MCTIMS USER MANUAL
2. SAT MANUAL Systems Approach to Training Manual

CDC-DESI-2017: Select Instructional Media

EVALUATION-CODED: NO   **SUSTAINMENT INTERVAL:** 24 months

GRADES: SGT, SSGT, GYSGT, MSGT, MGYSGT, WO-1, CWO-2, CWO-3, CWO-4, CWO-5, 2NDLT, 1STLT, CAPT, MAJ, LTCOL, COL

INITIAL TRAINING SETTING: FORMAL

CONDITION: Given Learning Objectives, Target Population Description, necessary materials and equipment, and with the aid of references

STANDARD: Consistent with the selected methods and adult learning preferences in accordance with the Systems Approach to Training (SAT) Manual chapter 2 section 2209 and SAT manual chapter 6

PERFORMANCE STEPS:
1. Review media considerations.
2. Record instructional media on the Learning Objective Worksheet (LOW).

REFERENCES:
1. MCTIMS USER MANUAL
2. SAT MANUAL Systems Approach to Training Manual

CDC-DESI-2018: Write Test Items

EVALUATION-CODED: NO   **SUSTAINMENT INTERVAL:** 24 months

GRADES: SGT, SSGT, GYSGT, MSGT, MGYSGT, WO-1, CWO-2, CWO-3, CWO-4, CWO-5, 2NDLT, 1STLT, CAPT, MAJ, LTCOL, COL

INITIAL TRAINING SETTING: FORMAL

CONDITION: Given Learning Analysis Worksheets (LAWs), Learning Objective Worksheets (LOWs), necessary materials and equipment, and with the aid of references.

STANDARD: Consistent with the Learning Objectives and their associated knowledge, skills, and attitudes in accordance with the Systems Approach to Training (SAT) Manual chapter 2 section 2207 and the SAT manual chapter 6.

PERFORMANCE STEPS:
1. Analyze the learning objective.
2. Determine test item type.
3. Write test item(s).
4. Record the test item(s) on the Learning Objective Worksheet (LOW).

REFERENCES:
1. MCTIMS USER MANUAL
2. SAT MANUAL Systems Approach to Training Manual

CDC-DESI-2019: Sequence Terminal Learning Objectives

EVALUATION-CODED: NO   **SUSTAINMENT INTERVAL**: 24 months

GRADES: SGT, SSGT, GYSGT, MSGT, MGYSGT, WO-1, CWO-2, CWO-3, CWO-4, CWO-5, 2NDLT, 1STLT, CAPT, MAJ, LTCOL, COL

INITIAL TRAINING SETTING: FORMAL

CONDITION: Given completed Learning Objective Worksheets (LOWs), necessary materials and equipment, and with the aid of references.

STANDARD: In a manner consistent with their relationships and that provides a structured learning progression in accordance with the Systems Approach to Training (SAT) Manual chapter 2 section 2300 and the SAT manual chapter 6.

PERFORMANCE STEPS:
1. Group Terminal Learning Objectives (TLOs) based on shared elements.
2. Determine relationship between Terminal Learning Objectives (TLOs).
3. Arrange Terminal Learning Objectives (TLOs) based upon relationships.

REFERENCES:
1. MCTIMS USER MANUAL
2. SAT MANUAL Systems Approach to Training Manual

CDC-DEVI-2012: Assemble a Master Lesson File

EVALUATION-CODED: NO   **SUSTAINMENT INTERVAL**: 24 months

GRADES: SGT, SSGT, GYSGT, MSGT, MGYSGT, WO-1, CWO-2, CWO-3, CWO-4, CWO-5, 2NDLT, 1STLT, CAPT, MAJ, LTCOL, COL

INITIAL TRAINING SETTING: FORMAL

CONDITION: Given Master Lesson File Components, necessary materials and equipment, and with the aid of references.

STANDARD: Ensuring all components are accurate per the master lesson file checklist in accordance with the Systems Approach to Training (SAT) Manual chapter 3 section 3800 and MCO 1553.2_.

PERFORMANCE STEPS:
1. Review MCO 1553.2A.
2. Review SOP for additional MLF requirement.
3. Gather required documents.
4. Complete the Master Lesson File (MLF) checklists.
5. Arrange documents in Master Lesson File (MLF).

REFERENCES:
1. MCO 1553.2A Management of Marine Corps Formal Schools and Training Detachments (Nov 03)
2. MCTIMS USER MANUAL
3. SAT MANUAL Systems Approach to Training Manual

CDC-DEVI-2020: Develop a Course Structure

EVALUATION-CODED: NO   **SUSTAINMENT INTERVAL:** 24 months

GRADES: SGT, SSGT, GYSGT, MSGT, MGYSGT, WO-1, CWO-2, CWO-3, CWO-4, CWO-5, 2NDLT, 1STLT, CAPT, MAJ, LTCOL, COL

INITIAL TRAINING SETTING: FORMAL

CONDITION: Given sequenced learning objectives, Standard Operating Procedures, necessary materials and equipment, and with the aid of references.

STANDARD: That establishes a strategy ensuring the components of all events are consistent with the sequenced terminal learning objectives, and in accordance with the Systems Approach to Training (SAT) Manual chapter 3 section 3100 and MCO 1553.2_.

PERFORMANCE STEPS:
1. Review source material.
2. Establish lessons content.
3. Establish exams content.
4. Estimate hours.
5. Assign titles.
6. Assign designators.

REFERENCES:
1. MCO 1553.2A Management of Marine Corps Formal Schools and Training Detachments (Nov 03)
2. MCTIMS USER MANUAL
3. SAT MANUAL Systems Approach to Training Manual

CDC-DEVI-2021: Develop Concept Cards

EVALUATION-CODED: NO   **SUSTAINMENT INTERVAL:** 24 months

GRADES: SGT, SSGT, GYSGT, MSGT, MGYSGT, WO-1, CWO-2, CWO-3, CWO-4, CWO-5, 2NDLT, 1STLT, CAPT, MAJ, LTCOL, COL

INITIAL TRAINING SETTING: FORMAL

CONDITION: Given a completed Learning Objective Worksheet (LOW), Course Structure, necessary materials and equipment, and with the aid of references.

STANDARD: Identifying all of the learning objectives, instructional methods and media, and the resources required to conduct the lesson, exam, or event, in accordance with the Systems Approach to Training (SAT) Manual chapter 3 section 3200

PERFORMANCE STEPS:
1. Determine categories of concept cards.
2. Identify methods from Learning Objective Worksheet.
3. Identify media from Learning Objective Worksheet.
4. Copy TLOs and ELOs from the Learning Objective Worksheet.
5. Identify support requirements for the assigned period of instruction.

REFERENCES:
1. MCO 1553.2A Management of Marine Corps Formal Schools and Training Detachments (Nov 03)
2. MCTIMS USER MANUAL
3. SAT MANUAL Systems Approach to Training Manual

CDC-DEVI-2022: Develop a Program of Instruction

EVALUATION-CODED: NO   **SUSTAINMENT INTERVAL**: 24 months

GRADES: SGT, SSGT, GYSGT, MSGT, MGYSGT, WO-1, CWO-2, CWO-3, CWO-4, CWO-5, 2NDLT, 1STLT, CAPT, MAJ, LTCOL, COL

INITIAL TRAINING SETTING: FORMAL

CONDITION: Given Standard Operating Procedures, necessary materials and equipment, and with the aid of references.

STANDARD: That describes resource requirements, course strategy, and evaluation procedures in accordance with the Systems Approach to Training (SAT) Manual chapter 3 section 3700 and MCO 1553.2.

PERFORMANCE STEPS:
1. Produce the Course Descriptive Data (CDD).
2. Complete the Program of Instruction (POI).

REFERENCES:
1. MCO 1553.2A Management of Marine Corps Formal Schools and Training Detachments (Nov 03)
2. MCTIMS USER MANUAL
3. SAT MANUAL Systems Approach to Training Manual

CDC-DEVI-2023: Construct a Test

EVALUATION-CODED: NO   SUSTAINMENT INTERVAL: 24 months

GRADES: SGT, SSGT, GYSGT, MSGT, MGYSGT, WO-1, CWO-2, CWO-3, CWO-4, CWO-5, 2NDLT, 1STLT, CAPT, MAJ, LTCOL, COL

INITIAL TRAINING SETTING: FORMAL

CONDITION: Given Learning Objective Worksheets (LOWs), Exam Concept Cards, an Operational Risk Assessment Worksheet (ORAW), necessary materials and equipment, and with the aid of references.

STANDARD: That determines student mastery of learning objectives associated with a specific exam concept card and utilizes the seven steps for constructing tests in accordance with the Systems Approach to Training (SAT) Manual chapter 3 section 3504.

PERFORMANCE STEPS:
1. Determine mastery.
2. Assigning test items
3. Arrange test items.
4. Develop grading criteria.
5. Develop scoring method.
6. Write testing instructions for student.
7. Write testing instructions for test administrators.

REFERENCES:
1. MCTIMS USER MANUAL
2. SAT MANUAL Systems Approach to Training Manual

CDC-DEVI-2024: Conduct Validation

EVALUATION-CODED: NO   SUSTAINMENT INTERVAL: 24 months

GRADES: SGT, SSGT, GYSGT, MSGT, MGYSGT, WO-1, CWO-2, CWO-3, CWO-4, CWO-5, 2NDLT, 1STLT, CAPT, MAJ, LTCOL, COL

INITIAL TRAINING SETTING: FORMAL

CONDITION: Given Standard Operating Procedures, the necessary materials and equipment, and with the aid of references.

STANDARD: To determine course validity that is consistent with the school Standard Operating Procedures, and in accordance with the Systems Approach to Training (SAT) Manual chapter 3 section 3600 and the SAT Manual chapter 5.

PERFORMANCE STEPS:
1. Review formal school/detachment SOP.
2. Plan validation.
3. Schedule validation.
4. Determine data collection procedures.
5. Implement validation plan.
6. Interpret validation results.

7. Record validation results.
8. Report validation results.

REFERENCES:
1. MCTIMS USER MANUAL
2. SAT MANUAL Systems Approach to Training Manual

CDC-DEVI-2025: Conduct an In-Depth Operational Risk Assessment

EVALUATION-CODED: NO   **SUSTAINMENT INTERVAL:** 24 months

GRADES: SGT, SSGT, GYSGT, MSGT, MGYSGT, WO-1, CWO-2, CWO-3, CWO-4, CWO-5, 2NDLT, 1STLT, CAPT, MAJ, LTCOL, COL

INITIAL TRAINING SETTING: FORMAL

CONDITION: Given completed Learning Analysis Worksheets (LAWs), Concept Cards, necessary materials and equipment, and with the aid of references.

STANDARD: To identify and assess hazards and implement controls to mitigate risk using the five-step process to mitigate potential hazards in accordance with the Systems Approach to Training (SAT) Manual chapter 3 section 3300 and MCO 3500.27B.

PERFORMANCE STEPS:
1. Identify hazards on Operational Risk Assessment Worksheet (ORAW).
2. Assess the hazards on Operational Risk Assessment Worksheet (ORAW).
3. Document how to implement controls on Operational Risk Assessment Worksheet (ORAW).
4. Document the supervision plan on Operational Risk Assessment Worksheet (ORAW).

REFERENCES:
1. MCO 1553.2A Management of Marine Corps Formal Schools and Training Detachments (Nov 03)
2. MCO 3500.27B Operational Risk Management (ORM) (MAY 2004)
3. MCO 5100.29A Marine Corps Safety Program (Jul 04)
4. MCTIMS USER MANUAL
5. SAT MANUAL Systems Approach to Training Manual

CDC-DEVI-2026: Write an Instructor Preparation Guide

EVALUATION-CODED: NO   **SUSTAINMENT INTERVAL:** 24 months

GRADES: SGT, SSGT, GYSGT, MSGT, MGYSGT, WO-1, CWO-2, CWO-3, CWO-4, CWO-5, 2NDLT, 1STLT, CAPT, MAJ, LTCOL, COL

INITIAL TRAINING SETTING: FORMAL

CONDITION: Given a Concept Card, Operational Risk Assessment Worksheet, Lesson Plan, Standard Operating Procedures, necessary materials and equipment, and with the aid of references.

STANDARD: That details the critical information required to instruct a lesson and is consistent with Master Lesson File components in accordance with the Systems Approach to Training (SAT) Manual chapter 3 section 3407.

PERFORMANCE STEPS:
1. Collect resources
2. Identify the components of the instructor preparation guide
3. Write an Instructor Preparation Guide.

REFERENCES:
1. SAT MANUAL Systems Approach to Training Manual

CDC-DEVI-2027: Write a Lesson Plan

EVALUATION-CODED: NO   **SUSTAINMENT INTERVAL**: 24 months

GRADES: SGT, SSGT, GYSGT, MSGT, MGYSGT, WO-1, CWO-2, CWO-3, CWO-4, CWO-5, 2NDLT, 1STLT, CAPT, MAJ, LTCOL, COL

INITIAL TRAINING SETTING: FORMAL

CONDITION: Given Learning Analysis Worksheets, Concept Card, Operational Risk Assessment Worksheet, necessary materials and equipment, and with the aid of references.

STANDARD: That details the strategy to be used in instructing a lesson and adheres to the established guidelines provided in the Systems Approach to Training (SAT) Manual chapter 3 section 3402.

PERFORMANCE STEPS:
1. Collect resources
2. Identify the parts that comprise a lesson plan
3. Identify the steps in writing a lesson plan
4. Write the introduction
5. Write the body
6. Write the summary

REFERENCES:
1. SAT MANUAL Systems Approach to Training Manual

CDC-DEVI-2028: Write Student Materials

EVALUATION-CODED: NO   **SUSTAINMENT INTERVAL**: 24 months

GRADES: SGT, SSGT, GYSGT, MSGT, MGYSGT, WO-1, CWO-2, CWO-3, CWO-4, CWO-5, 2NDLT, 1STLT, CAPT, MAJ, LTCOL, COL

INITIAL TRAINING SETTING: FORMAL

CONDITION: Given a Lesson Plan, necessary materials and equipment, and with the aid of references.

STANDARD: That follow the conceptual framework established in the Lesson Plan and support the instruction of learning objectives in accordance with the Systems Approach to Training (SAT) Manual chapter 3 section 3403.

PERFORMANCE STEPS:
1. Collect resources
2. Identify the types of student outlines
3. Identify the components of a student outline
4. Develop student outline
5. Develop supplemental materials

REFERENCES:
1. SAT MANUAL Systems Approach to Training Manual

CDC-DEVI-2029: Develop Instructional Media

EVALUATION-CODED: NO   **SUSTAINMENT INTERVAL:** 24 months

GRADES: SGT, SSGT, GYSGT, MSGT, MGYSGT, WO-1, CWO-2, CWO-3, CWO-4, CWO-5, 2NDLT, 1STLT, CAPT, MAJ, LTCOL, COL

INITIAL TRAINING SETTING: FORMAL

CONDITION: Given a Lesson Plan, necessary materials and equipment, and with the aid of references.

STANDARD: That supports the Lesson Plan content and is consistent with media development considerations established in the Systems Approach to Training (SAT) Manual chapter 3 sections 3404-3405.

PERFORMANCE STEPS:
1. Collect resources
2. Identify the types of media
3. Identify media development considerations
4. Develop board media
5. Develop projected media
6. Develop established media

REFERENCES:
1. SAT MANUAL Systems Approach to Training Manual

CDC-TIMS-2011: Use the Automated System in Curriculum Development

EVALUATION-CODED: NO   **SUSTAINMENT INTERVAL:** 24 months

GRADES: SGT, SSGT, GYSGT, MSGT, MGYSGT, WO-1, CWO-2, CWO-3, CWO-4, CWO-5, 2NDLT, 1STLT, CAPT, MAJ, LTCOL

INITIAL TRAINING SETTING: FORMAL

CONDITION: Given MCTIMS access, developed course data, necessary materials and equipment, and with the aid of references.

STANDARD: By recording data consistent with previously established academic products in accordance with MCTIMS Users Manual and chapters 2 and 3 of the SAT Manual.

PERFORMANCE STEPS:
1. Navigate through MCTIMS.
2. Enter data into MCTIMS.
3. Print MCTIMS reports.
4. Exit MCTIMS.

REFERENCES:
1. MCO 1553.3A Unit Training Management (UTM) (Jan 04)
2. MCTIMS USER MANUAL
3. SAT MANUAL Systems Approach to Training Manual

T3 T&R MANUAL

CHAPTER 5

FORMAL SCHOOL MANAGEMENT INDIVIDUAL EVENTS

	PARAGRAPH	PAGE
PURPOSE	5000	5-2
ADMINISTRATIVE NOTES.	5001	5-2
INDEX OF INDIVIDUAL EVENTS.	5002	5-3
2000-LEVEL EVENTS	5003	5-4

T3 T&R MANUAL

CHAPTER 5

FORMAL SCHOOL MANAGEMENT INDIVIDUAL EVENTS

5000. PURPOSE. This chapter details the individual events that pertain to the T3 community. These events are linked to designated formal school Mission Essential Tasks (MET). This linkage tailor's individual training for the selected MET. Each individual event provides an event title, along with the conditions events will be performed under, and the standard to which the event must be performed to be successful.

5001. ADMINISTRATIVE NOTES. T&R events are coded for ease of reference. Each event has a 4-4-4 digit identifier. The first four digits represent the occupational field or military occupational field (FSIC, URP, or FSM). The second four digits represent the functional or duty area (ANLZ, DESI, etc.). The last four digits represent the level, and identifier number of the event. Every individual event has an identifier number from 001 to 999.

5002. INDEX OF INDIVIDUAL EVENTS

EVENT	TITLE	PAGE
	2000 LEVEL EVENTS	
FSM-ANLZ-2001	Develop a T&R Event	5-4
FSM-DESI-2006	Integrate Adult Learning Theory into Curriculum Development	5-4
FSM-EVLI-2007	Implement a Formal School Evaluation Plan	5-5
FSM-EVLI-2008	Assist in a Course Content Review Board (CCRB)	5-5
FSM-MANI-2002	Implement Formal School Academic Standard Operating Procedure	5-6
FSM-MANI-2003	Implement a Staff and Faculty Development Plan	5-6
FSM-MANI-2004	Develop Memorandum of Agreement/Understanding	5-7
FSM-MANI-2005	Conduct Operational Risk Management	5-7
FSM-TIMS-2009	Administrate the Use of MCTIMS	5-8

5003. 2000-LEVEL EVENTS

FSM-ANLZ-2001: Develop a T&R Event

EVALUATION-CODED: NO   **SUSTAINMENT INTERVAL:** 24 months

INITIAL TRAINING SETTING: FORMAL

CONDITION: Given Subject Matter Experts, MCTIMS, scenario, and references.

STANDARD: In accordance with T&R Program Order 3500.72A chapter 4.

PERFORMANCE STEPS:
1. Review existing T&R Events
2. Specify references
3. Analyze Operating Force job requirements
4. Create the task behavior
5. Create the condition
6. Create the standard
7. Create the Performance Steps/Component Events
8. Determine sustainment interval
9. Determine billets or grades performing
10. Determine training setting
11. Determine E-Coded or nonE-Coded
12. Determine any administrative notes for performance steps
13. Determine resource requirements

REFERENCES:
1. MCO 1553.2A Management of Marine Corps Formal Schools and Training Detachments (Nov 03)
2. MCO 3500.19B Training and Readiness Manual
3. MCTIMS USER MANUAL
4. SAT MANUAL Systems Approach to Training Manual

FSM-DESI-2006: Integrate Adult Learning Theory into Curriculum Development

EVALUATION-CODED: NO   **SUSTAINMENT INTERVAL:** 24 months

INITIAL TRAINING SETTING: MOJT

CONDITION: Given program of instruction to develop, a Target Population Description (TPD), instructional materials, curriculum developers, and references.

STANDARD: To produce curriculum that is tailored to meet different learner's needs and in accordance with the Systems Approach to Training (SAT) Manual chapters 2, 3 and 6.

PERFORMANCE STEPS:
1. Apply Adult Learning Theory (ALT) to writing learning objectives.
2. Apply Adult Learning Theory (ALT) to writing test items.
3. Apply Adult Learning Theory (ALT) to selecting instructional methods.
4. Apply Adult Learning Theory (ALT) to selecting instructional media.

REFERENCES:
1. SAT MANUAL Systems Approach to Training Manual

FSM-EVLI-2007: Implement a Formal School Evaluation Plan

EVALUATION-CODED: NO   SUSTAINMENT INTERVAL: 24 months

INITIAL TRAINING SETTING: FORMAL

CONDITION: Given a formal school and references

STANDARD: in accordance with the Systems Approach to Training (SAT) Manual chapter 5 and MCO 1553.2A.

PERFORMANCE STEPS:
1. Determine evaluation requirements
2. Design formal school evaluation plan
3. Collect Data
4. Analyze Data
5. Recommend changes

REFERENCES:
1. SAT MANUAL Systems Approach to Training Manual

MISCELLANEOUS:

ADMINISTRATIVE INSTRUCTIONS: School and Detachment are interchangeable. Collecting, analyzing, and evaluating pertinent data to determine the effectiveness and efficiency of an instructional program and to make recommendations for use by decision-makers to modify, continue, or terminate a program, in accordance with Chapter 5 of the SAT Manual & MCO 1553.2A.

FSM-EVLI-2008: Assist in a Course Content Review Board (CCRB)

EVALUATION-CODED: NO   SUSTAINMENT INTERVAL: 24 months

INITIAL TRAINING SETTING: FORMAL

CONDITION: Given the course materials, evaluation data, and Subject Matter Experts (SMEs), and references.

STANDARD: To determine course content requirements in accordance with the Systems Approach to Training (SAT) Manual chapter 5 section 5500.

PERFORMANCE STEPS:
1. Plan the CCRB
2. Assist in the analyze phase
3. Assist in the design phase
4. Assist in the develop phase
5. Assist in developing the Record of Proceedings (ROP)
6. Develop the POI deficiencies letter

REFERENCES:
1. MCO 1553.2A Management of Marine Corps Formal Schools and Training
    Detachments (Nov 03)
2. SAT MANUAL Systems Approach to Training Manual

FSM-MANI-2002: Implement Formal School Academic Standard Operating Procedure

EVALUATION-CODED: NO   **SUSTAINMENT INTERVAL:** 24 months

INITIAL TRAINING SETTING: FORMAL

CONDITION: Given a formal school, commander's intent, evaluation plan, staff
and faculty development plan, and references.

STANDARD: To achieve the commander's intent regarding academic policies
within the formal school and in accordance with MCO 1553.2_.

PERFORMANCE STEPS:
1. Review policies and procedures for formal schools
2. Determine formal school academic SOP requirements
3. Develop formal school academic SOP
4. Integrate evaluation plan
5. Integrate staff and faculty development plan
6. Publish formal school academic SOP

REFERENCES:
1. MCO 1553.2A Management of Marine Corps Formal Schools and Training
    Detachments (Nov 03)
2. SAT MANUAL Systems Approach to Training Manual

FSM-MANI-2003: Implement a Staff and Faculty Development Plan

EVALUATION-CODED: NO   **SUSTAINMENT INTERVAL:** 24 months

DESCRIPTION: 1. Improve teaching; 2. Maintain current academic technical
knowledge and skills; 3. In-service training for vocation education and
employment training programs; 4. Retraining to meet changing institutional
needs; 5. Intersegmental exchange programs; 6. Development of innovations in
instructional and administrative techniques and program effectiveness; 7.
Computer and technological proficiency programs; 8. Other activities
determined to be related to educational and professional development.

INITIAL TRAINING SETTING: FORMAL

CONDITION: Given formal school staff/faculty, commander's intent, and
references.

STANDARD: To achieve the commander's intent regarding staff and faculty
development within the formal school and in accordance with MCO 1553.2A.

PERFORMANCE STEPS:
1. Determine staff/faculty experience
2. Determine development requirements

3. Develop staff/faculty development plan
4. Publish the formal school staff/faculty development plan

REFERENCES:
1. AIRS-400 Checklist
2. MCO 1553.2A Management of Marine Corps Formal Schools and Training Detachments (Nov 03)

MISCELLANEOUS:

ADMINISTRATIVE INSTRUCTIONS: 1. Improve teaching. 2. Maintain current academic technical knowledge and skills. 3. In-service training for vocation education and employment training programs. 4. Retraining to meet changing institutional needs. 5. Intersegmental exchange programs. 6. Development of innovations in instructional and administrative techniques and program effectiveness. 7. Computer and technological proficiency programs. 8. Other activities determined to be related to educational and professional development.

FSM-MANI-2004: Develop Memorandum of Agreement / Understanding

EVALUATION-CODED: NO   **SUSTAINMENT INTERVAL:** 24 months

INITIAL TRAINING SETTING: MOJT

CONDITION: Given a formal school, a host command, and references.

STANDARD: To facilitate the use of resources and logistical support between host and tenant command.

PERFORMANCE STEPS:
1. Establish range/training area requirements
2. Establish facilities support
3. Establish logistical support
4. Ensure all MOAs/MOUs are current
5. Ensure all MOAs/MOUs are submitted for approval
6. Coordinate consolidated submissions as required

REFERENCES:
1. AIRS-400 Checklist
2. MCO 1553.2A Management of Marine Corps Formal Schools and Training Detachments (Nov 03)

FSM-MANI-2005: Conduct Operational Risk Management

EVALUATION-CODED: NO   **SUSTAINMENT INTERVAL:** 24 months

INITIAL TRAINING SETTING: MOJT

CONDITION: Given a formal school, a POI(s), personnel, and references.

STANDARD: To minimize risk and mitigate hazards in the operation of a formal school.

PERFORMANCE STEPS:
1. Gather appropriate resources
2. Review all courses to determine if they are high-risk training
3. Review current ORM Plans
4. Review current Operational Risk Assessment Worksheets (ORAW)
5. Update ORAs on an annual basis
6. Ensure MLFs are current, IAW ORAW changes
7. Determine High-risk personnel requirements

REFERENCES:
1. MCO 3500.27B Operational Risk Management (ORM) (MAY 2004)
2. MCO 5100.29A Marine Corps Safety Program (Jul 04)
3. SAT MANUAL Systems Approach to Training Manual

FSM-TIMS-2009: Administrate the Use of MCTIMS

EVALUATION-CODED: YES   **SUSTAINMENT INTERVAL:** 1 month

INITIAL TRAINING SETTING: MOJT

CONDITION: Given MCTIMS access, an academics staff, and references.

STANDARD: In accordance with TECOM directives and the MCTIMS user manual.

PERFORMANCE STEPS:
1. Ensure the use of MCTIMS Student Registrar module
2. Ensure the use of use MCTIMS Student Management module
3. Ensure the use of MCTIMS Curriculum Management module
4. Ensure the use of MCTIMS Training and Readiness Manual module
5. Ensure the use of MCTIMS student evaluation module
6. Ensure the use of MCTIMS to produce reports as required

REFERENCES:
1. MCTIMS USER MANUAL
2. SAT MANUAL Systems Approach to Training Manual

T3 T&R MANUAL

CHAPTER 6

UNIT READINESS PLANNING (URP) INDIVIDUAL EVENTS

	PARAGRAPH	PAGE
PURPOSE	6000	6-2
ADMINISTRATIVE NOTES.	6001	6-2
INDEX OF INDIVIDUAL EVENTS.	6002	6-3
2000-LEVEL EVENTS	6003	6-4

T3 T&R MANUAL

CHAPTER 6

UNIT READINESS PLANNING (URP) INDIVIDUAL EVENTS

6000. PURPOSE. This chapter details the individual events that pertain to the T3 community. These events are linked to designated formal school Mission Essential Tasks (MET). This linkage tailor's individual training for the selected MET. Each individual event provides an event title, along with the conditions events will be performed under, and the standard to which the event must be performed to be successful.

6001. ADMINISTRATIVE NOTES. T&R events are coded for ease of reference. Each event has a 4-4-4 digit identifier. The first four digits represent the occupational field or military occupational field (URP, or FSIC). The second four digits represent the functional or duty area (ANLZ, DESI, etc.). The last four digits represent the level, and identifier number of the event. Every individual event has an identifier number from 001 to 999.

6002. INDEX OF INDIVIDUAL EVENTS

EVENT	TITLE	PAGE
	2000 LEVEL EVENTS	
URP-ANLZ-2001	Develop METL	6-4
URP-DESI-2006	Conduct Training Assessment	6-4
URP-DESI-2007	Determine Training Strategy	6-5
URP-DESI-2008	Develop Training Guidance	6-6
URP-DESI-2009	Develop a Long Range Training Plan	6-7
URP-DESI-2010	Develop a Mid Range Training Plan	6-7
URP-DESI-2011	Develop a Short Range Training Plan	6-9
URP-DESI-2012	Develop Training Schedules	6-10
URP-DEVI-2016	Coordinate Unit Training	6-11
URP-DEVI-2017	Prepare for Training	6-11
URP-DEVI-2019	Conduct Operational Risk Assessment	6-12
URP-ELVI-2015	Conduct After-Action Reviews	6-12
URP-ELVI-2028	Evaluate Training	6-13
URP-IMPI-2024	Conduct Training	6-14

6003. 2000-LEVEL EVENTS

URP-ANLZ-2001: Develop METL

EVALUATION-CODED: NO   **SUSTAINMENT INTERVAL:** 24 months

GRADES: SGT, SSGT, GYSGT, MSGT, MAJ, LTCOL, COL

INITIAL TRAINING SETTING: FORMAL

CONDITION: Given a Table of Organization (T/O) mission, Core METs from the T&R Manual, HHQ METL and commander's guidance, Marine Corps Task List (MCTL), any additional essential tasking(s) (Named Operations, Operations and/or Contingency Plan), a unit to train, and references.

STANDARD: Within 45 days, that is approved by the Higher Headquarter's Commander.

PERFORMANCE STEPS:
1. Receive/Analyze HHQ Mission and METL
2. Review the unit's Table of Organization (T/O) Mission Statement
3. List Core METs from the unit's Training and Readiness (T&R) Manual
4. Determine any additional essential tasks (From O/Con Plans, Named Operations, War Plans, etc)
5. Tie METs to Marine Corps Task List (MCTL) identification number (ex: MCT: 1.3.5)
6. Revise/Restate unit mission statement, as applicable
7. Submit Draft METL and Mission statement to next Higher Headquarter's commander for approval
8. Publish the approved METL

REFERENCES:
1. Army FM-101 Battle Focused Training (sept 90)
2. MCO 1553.3A Unit Training Management (UTM) (Jan 04)
3. MCRP 3-0A Unit Training Management Guide (Nov 96)
4. MCRP 3-0B How to Conduct Training (Nov 96)

URP-DESI-2006: Conduct Training Assessment

EVALUATION-CODED: NO   **SUSTAINMENT INTERVAL:** 24 months

GRADES: SSGT, GYSGT, 1STSGT, MSGT, MGYSGT, SGTMAJ, WO-1, CWO-2, CWO-3, CWO-4, CWO-5, 2NDLT, 1STLT, CAPT, MAJ, LTCOL, COL

INITIAL TRAINING SETTING: FORMAL

CONDITION: Given a Mission Essential Task List (METL) and mission statement, Higher Headquarters METL and commander's guidance, a unit to train, training and readiness manual(s), references, and using evaluation/assessment data.

STANDARD: To determine proficiency/deficiency in each MET within 90 days of assuming command.

PERFORMANCE STEPS:
1. Analyze evaluation data.
2. Assess unit proficiencies/strengths
3. Assess unit deficiencies/weaknesses
4. Determine Opportunities for the unit
5. Determine Threats that may affect the unit

REFERENCES:
1. Army FM-101 Battle Focused Training (Sep 90)
2. MCO 1553.3A Unit Training Management (UTM) (Jan 04)
3. MCRP 3-0A Unit Training Management Guide (Nov 96)
4. MCRP 3-0B How to Conduct Training (Nov 96)

MISCELLANEOUS:

ADMINISTRATIVE INSTRUCTIONS: Subordinate unit leaders should be involved in the execution of this task whenever possible.

URP-DESI-2007: Determine Training Strategy

EVALUATION-CODED: NO   **SUSTAINMENT INTERVAL:** 24 months

GRADES: SGT, SSGT, GYSGT, 1STSGT, MSGT, SGTMAJ, MGYSGT, WO-1, CWO-2, CWO-3, CWO-4, CWO-5, 2NDLT, 1STLT, CAPT, MAJ, LTCOL, COL

INITIAL TRAINING SETTING: FORMAL

CONDITION: Given an approved Mission Essential Task List (METL) and mission statement, HHQ METL and commander's guidance, a unit to train, training and readiness (T&R) manual(s), PTP/Formal/Ancillary Requirements, unit training assessment, and references.

STANDARD: Which generates training priorities to achieve and sustain proficiency in each MET.

PERFORMANCE STEPS:
1. Employ training assessment findings.
2. Establish training priorities
3. Specify "E" Coded events
4. Sequence training events and objectives
5. Specify frequency that each MET will be performed during the upcoming training period
6. Plan for re-training tasks not performed to standard
7. Determine resource requirements
8. Issue guidance that links the METL to Training Exercises
9. Outline the unit training vision and philosophy

REFERENCES:
1. Army FM-101 Battle Focused Training (sept 90)
2. MCO 1553.3A Unit Training Management (UTM) (Jan 04)
3. MCRP 3-0A Unit Training Management Guide (Nov 96)
4. MCRP 3-0B How to Conduct Training (Nov 96)

MISCELLANEOUS:

ADMINISTRATIVE INSTRUCTIONS: 1. Subordinate unit leaders should be involved in the execution of this task whenever possible. 2. Report resource shortfalls to higher headquarters. 3. Commander's must weigh all training requirements as part of the training strategy including mission-oriented, formal, ancillary, pre-deployment training, professional military education, and Marine Corps Common Skills.

URP-DESI-2008: Develop Training Guidance

EVALUATION-CODED: NO   **SUSTAINMENT INTERVAL:** 24 months

DESCRIPTION: Examples of topics normally addressed in the CTG are: Unit METL & Mission Statement Commanders assessment of METL proficiency. Training Goals. Training priorities and strategy to improve and sustain METL proficiency. Major training events/exercises and associated training standards combined arms training. Pre-Deployment Training Program requirements. Formal & Ancillary Training Requirements Organizational inspection program. A cross-reference of training events and associated METL training objectives. Collective and Individual training. Leader development and leader training. Self-development. Preparation/Training of trainers and evaluators. Training evaluation and feedback. Force integration. Resource allocation and guidance. Training management. Risk management. New equipment training, as applicable Joint, Interagency, Intergovernmental, and Multinational (JIIM) training, as applicable.

GRADES: CWO-2, CWO-3, CWO-4, CWO-5, CAPT, MAJ, LTCOL, COL

INITIAL TRAINING SETTING: FORMAL

CONDITION: Given a Mission Essential Task List (METL) and mission statement, commander's guidance, a unit to train, training and readiness (T&R) manual(s), collective training events, a unit training assessment, a training strategy and references.

STANDARD: To publish a training guidance letter that focuses unit training on MET proficiency and ensures unity of effort toward unit readiness training in accordance with the commander's training priorities and the references.

PERFORMANCE STEPS:
1. Review training strategy.
2. Identify unit combat readiness requirements
3. Determine operational risk assessment requirements
4. Determine Commander's End-state
5. Specify Training Milestones
6. Specify Subordinate tasks
7. Specify Coordinating Instructions
8. Specify Administrative Requirements
9. Specify Logistical Requirements
10. Specify Command and Control Requirements
11. Create Commander's Training Guidance Letter incorporating the major elements (listed in "Description" section of this T&R Event above)
12. Publish Commander's Training Guidance Letter

REFERENCES:
1. Army FM-101 Battle Focused Training (Sep 90)
2. MCO 1553.3A Unit Training Management (UTM) (Jan 04)
3. MCRP 3-0A Unit Training Management Guide (Nov 96)
4. MCRP 3-0B How to Conduct Training (Nov 96)

URP-DESI-2009: Develop a Long Range Training Plan

EVALUATION-CODED: NO   **SUSTAINMENT INTERVAL:** 24 months

GRADES: GYSGT, 1STSGT, MSGT, MGYSGT, SGTMAJ, CWO-2, CWO-3, CWO-4, CWO-5, 2NDLT, 1STLT, CAPT, MAJ, LTCOL, COL

INITIAL TRAINING SETTING: FORMAL

CONDITION: Given a Training Plan with corresponding TEEP from Higher Headquarters, a Mission Essential Task List (METL) and mission statement, a unit to train, training and readiness (T&R) manual(s), a unit training assessment, a training strategy, the commander's training guidance, and references.

STANDARD: That includes the unit mission and METL, commander's training guidance, a calendar/TEEP that identifies major exercises, deployments, and other known training requirements in a designated 12-24 month time period, and identifies training resource requirements, in accordance with the UTM Best Practices Guide and MCRP 3-0A, Chapter 6, section 2.

PERFORMANCE STEPS:
1. Incorporate Commander's Training Guidance into the plan
2. Include the Unit METL and Mission Statement
3. Identify Major Training events and exercises
4. Graphically display major unit activities (Calendar/TEEP)
5. Prioritize Formal, Ancillary and Pre-Deployment Training Plan (PTP) training requirements
6. Determine open training time (white space)
7. Allocate Resources
8. Issue long range training plan to subordinates.

REFERENCES:
1. Army FM-101 Battle Focused Training (Sep 90)
2. MCO 1553.3A Unit Training Management (UTM) (Jan 04)
3. MCRP 3-0A Unit Training Management Guide (Nov 96)
4. MCRP 3-0B How to Conduct Training (Nov 96)

URP-DESI-2010: Develop a Mid Range Training Plan

EVALUATION-CODED: NO   **SUSTAINMENT INTERVAL:** 24 months

DESCRIPTION: Properly developed training plans will: -Maintain a consistent combat focus. Each headquarters in the organization involves its subordinate headquarters in the development of training plans. Based on HHQs plan, the subordinate commanders prepare plans that have a consistent combat focus throughout the unit. -Coordinate between associated combat, combat support, and CSS organizations. MAGTF commanders plan for coordinated combined-arms and Services training of their task organizations. All MAGTF component commanders actively participate in this process and develop complementary training plans. MAGTF commanders require integrated training plans and must monitor and coordinate their efforts with component commanders during the planning process. -Focus on real world lead times. Training plans must reflect real - world lead times required to cause desired effects. If commanders want to influence fiscal year program objective memorandum, their long-range plans must be submitted to the appropriate headquarters in enough time for that headquarters to incorporate the planning requirements into the budget process. Commanders must look ahead to unit deployment program rotations, deployments, major exercises, and budget cycles and then provide appropriate guidance in their planning process. -Address future proficiency. Training plans must focus on raising or sustaining proficiency in METs. -Use resources efficiently. Since time and resources are limited, the planning process must identify and effectively allocate time and resources needed to achieve and sustain combat proficiency.

GRADES: SGT, SSGT, GYSGT, 1STSGT, MSGT, SGTMAJ, MGYSGT, CWO-2, CWO-3, CWO-4, CWO-5, 2NDLT, 1STLT, CAPT, MAJ, LTCOL, COL

INITIAL TRAINING SETTING: FORMAL

CONDITION: Given a Mission Essential Task List (METL) and mission statement, a unit to train, training and readiness (T&R) manual(s), a unit training assessment, a training strategy, commander's training guidance, Long range training plans, and references.

STANDARD: To convert the long-range training plan into a 4 -12 month plan that is a series of training activities and events, issuing detailed commanders training guidance, allocating and coordinating training resources, and validating the training plan, in accordance with MCRP 3-0A, Chapter 6, Section 3.

PERFORMANCE STEPS:
1. Review current unit proficiency/resources/training environment.
2. State unit METL and mission statement
3. Incorporate commanders training guidance.
4. Extract pertinent information from the long-range training plan.
5. Review previous midrange plans.
6. Incorporate major training and operational activities/events
7. Develop midrange planning calendar.
8. Link Collective Training Events (CTEs) to METs
9. Identify "E" Coded events
10. Coordinate with higher/subordinate units.
11. Issue the midrange training plan to subordinates.
12. Update the midrange training plan, as required.

REFERENCES:
1. Army FM-101 Battle Focused Training (sept 90)
2. MCO 1553.3A Unit Training Management (UTM) (Jan 04)
3. MCRP 3-0A Unit Training Management Guide (Nov 96)
4. MCRP 3-0B How to Conduct Training (Nov 96)

URP-DESI-2011: Develop a Short Range Training Plan

EVALUATION-CODED: NO   SUSTAINMENT INTERVAL: 24 months

DESCRIPTION: Properly developed training plans will: -Maintain a consistent combat focus. Each headquarters in the organization involves its subordinate headquarters in the development of training plans. Based on HHQs plan, the subordinate commanders prepare plans that have a consistent combat focus throughout the unit. -Coordinate between associated combat, combat support, and CSS organizations. MAGTF commanders plan for coordinated combined-arms and Services training of their task organizations. All MAGTF component commanders actively participate in this process and develop complementary training plans. MAGTF commanders require integrated training plans and must monitor and coordinate their efforts with component commanders during the planning process. -Focus on real world lead times. Training plans must reflect real - world lead times required to cause desired effects. If commanders want to influence fiscal year program objective memorandum, their long-range plans must be submitted to the appropriate headquarters in enough time for that headquarters to incorporate the planning requirements into the budget process. Commanders must look ahead to unit deployment program rotations, deployments, major exercises, and budget cycles and then provide appropriate guidance in their planning process. -Address future proficiency. Training plans must focus on raising or sustaining proficiency in METs.-Use resources efficiently. Since time and resources are limited, the planning process must identify and effectively allocate time and resources needed to achieve and sustain combat proficiency.

GRADES: SGT, SSGT, GYSGT, MSGT, MGYSGT, CWO-2, CWO-3, CWO-4, CWO-5, 2NDLT, 1STLT, CAPT, MAJ, LTCOL, COL

INITIAL TRAINING SETTING: FORMAL

CONDITION: Given a Mission Essential Task List (METL) and mission statement, a unit to train, training and readiness (T&R) manual (s), a unit training assessment, a training strategy, commander's training guidance, existing training plans, and references.

STANDARD: To convert the mid-range training plan into a 1-4 month plan that is a series of training activities and events, issuing detailed commanders training guidance, allocating and coordinating training resources, and validating the training plan, in accordance with MCRP 3-0A, Chapter 6, Section 3.

PERFORMANCE STEPS:
1. State Unit METL and mission
2. Incorporate the Commander's Training Guidance
3. Determine requirements from the mid range training plan.
4. Review the previous Short Range Plan
5. Link collective and individual training standards to training events.
6. Specify major training activities and events.
7. Determine training locations.
8. Determine logistical requirements.
9. Specify training dates.
10. Determine training events.
11. Determine unit (s)/personnel participating in the training events.

12. Update training plans, as required.
13. Specify tasks for each sub-unit and staff section
14. Specify time line for completion of all training requirements
15. Issue the short range training plan to subordinates.

REFERENCES:
1. Army FM-101 Battle Focused Training (Sep 90)
2. MCO 1553.3A Unit Training Management (UTM) (Jan 04)
3. MCRP 3-0A Unit Training Management Guide (Nov 96)
4. MCRP 3-0B How to Conduct Training (Nov 96)

URP-DESI-2012: Develop Training Schedules

EVALUATION-CODED: NO   SUSTAINMENT INTERVAL: 24 months

DESCRIPTION: Training Schedules can be for any length of time: Daily, Weekly, Monthly, etc. A Training Schedule provides specific guidance for each scheduled event to include, when and where training takes place, collective and individual training standards applicable to the event, designation of supervisors/trainers/evaluators, required gear and uniform, transportation, and safety precautions, in accordance with the references.

GRADES: CPL, SGT, SSGT, GYSGT, MSGT, MGYSGT, WO-1, CWO-2, CWO-3, CWO-4, CWO-5, 2NDLT, 1STLT, CAPT, MAJ, LTCOL, COL

INITIAL TRAINING SETTING: FORMAL

CONDITION: Given a Mission Essential Task List (METL) and mission statement, a Unit Training Plan, a unit to train, training and readiness (T&R) manual(s), commander's training guidance, and references.

STANDARD: To include all the required information to conduct the specified training, in accordance with MCRP 3-0A, Chapter 6, Section 4.

PERFORMANCE STEPS:
1. Specify when training starts
2. Specify training and training related locations
3. Allocate adequate time for scheduled training and additional training as required to correct anticipated deficiencies
4. Specify individual, leader/MCCS, and collective tasks to be trained
5. Provide concurrent/"hip pocket" training topics that will efficiently use available training time
6. Specify who conducts the training and who evaluates the training
7. Provide administrative information concerning uniform, weapon, equipment, references, and safety precautions
8. Specify training activity(s)/event(s) to be conducted.
9. Specify remediation/recovery details
10. Issue the schedule to HHQ & Subordinates

REFERENCES:
1. Army FM-101 Battle Focused Training (Sep 90)
2. MCO 1553.3A Unit Training Management (UTM) (Jan 04)
3. MCRP 3-0A Unit Training Management Guide (Nov 96)
4. MCRP 3-0B How to Conduct Training (Nov 96)

URP-DEVI-2016: Coordinate Unit Training

EVALUATION-CODED: NO   **SUSTAINMENT INTERVAL:** 24 months

GRADES: CPL, SGT, SSGT, GYSGT, MSGT, MGYSGT, WO-1, CWO-2, CWO-3, CWO-4, CWO-5, 2NDLT, 1STLT, CAPT, MAJ, LTCOL, COL

INITIAL TRAINING SETTING: FORMAL

CONDITION: Given the commanders training guidance, T&R Manuals, training plans, training schedules, and references.

STANDARD: Addressing the five W's, {who, what, where, when, and why} for each training event to provide the requisite level of support necessary for successful training per the commander's guidance.

PERFORMANCE STEPS:
1. Develop & Publish the Letter of Instruction (LOI)
2. Confirm trainers and support personnel.
3. Allocate resources.
4. Conduct Operational Risk Management using the ORAW
5. Conduct reconnaissance of training areas.
6. Coordinate with adjacent units and appropriate personnel.
7. Inspect equipment.
8. Develop and Publish the Training Support Request (TSR)
9. Resolve training conflicts and shortfalls.
10. Update training plans and schedules as required.
11. Conduct Range/Training Area Reconnaissance.
12. Follow up on supported requested in the TSR

REFERENCES:
1. Army FM-101 Battle Focused Training (sept 90)
2. MCO 1553.3A Unit Training Management (UTM) (Jan 04)
3. MCRP 3-0A Unit Training Management Guide (Nov 96)
4. MCRP 3-0B How to Conduct Training (Nov 96)

MISCELLANEOUS:

  ADMINISTRATIVE INSTRUCTIONS: 1. LOI's are published in the operational format OSMEAC

URP-DEVI-2017: Prepare for Training

EVALUATION-CODED: NO   **SUSTAINMENT INTERVAL:** 24 months

GRADES: CPL, SGT, SSGT, GYSGT, 1STSGT, MSGT, MGYSGT, SGTMAJ, WO-1, CWO-2, CWO-3, CWO-4, CWO-5, 2NDLT, 1STLT, CAPT, MAJ, LTCOL, COL

INITIAL TRAINING SETTING: FORMAL

CONDITION: Given a Training Plan and/or Training schedule, T&R Manual, and a unit to train.

STANDARD: To ensure that trainers, evaluators, leaders and participants are certified to execute the training activity to established standard.

PERFORMANCE STEPS:
1. Select Trainers
2. Create/Obtain Training materials
3. Prepare Trainers
4. Create Performance Checklist
5. Conduct a Confirmation Brief
6. Conduct Rehearsals

REFERENCES:
1. Army FM-101 Battle Focused Training (Sep 90)
2. MCRP 3-0A Unit Training Management Guide (Nov 96)
3. MCTIMS Instructions Marine Corps Training Information Management System (MCTIMS) Instructions
4. SAT MANUAL Systems Approach to Training Manual

URP-DEVI-2019: Conduct Operational Risk Assessment

EVALUATION-CODED: NO   **SUSTAINMENT INTERVAL**: 24 months

GRADES: CPL, SGT, SSGT, GYSGT, 1STSGT, MSGT, MGYSGT, SGTMAJ, WO-1, CWO-2, CWO-3, CWO-4, CWO-5, 2NDLT, 1STLT, CAPT, MAJ, LTCOL, COL

INITIAL TRAINING SETTING: MOJT

CONDITION: Given an Operational Risk Assessment Worksheet (ORAW), training materials, training plan, and with the aid of references.

STANDARD: To mitigate risks associated with each training event by identifying and incorporating control measures through the Operational Risk Assessment Worksheet (ORAW) in accordance with the references.

PERFORMANCE STEPS:
1. Identify hazards.
2. Assess hazards.
3. Make risk decisions.
4. Implement controls to mitigate risk.
5. Supervise training.
6. Assess effectiveness of control measures.
7. Develop ORAW for every training event.

REFERENCES:
1. MCO 1553.3A Unit Training Management (UTM) (Jan 04)
2. MCO 3500.27B Operational Risk Management (ORM) (MAY 2004)
3. MCRP 3-0A Unit Training Management Guide (Nov 96)
4. SAT MANUAL Systems Approach to Training Manual

URP-EVLI-2015: Conduct After-Action Reviews (AAR)

EVALUATION-CODED: NO   **SUSTAINMENT INTERVAL**: 24 months

GRADES: CPL, SGT, SSGT, GYSGT, 1STSGT, MSGT, MGYSGT, SGTMAJ, WO-1, CWO-2, CWO-3, CWO-4, CWO-5, 2NDLT, 1STLT, CAPT, MAJ, LTCOL

INITIAL TRAINING SETTING: FORMAL

CONDITION: Given a training event/activity, unit to train, evaluation data, trend analysis, and with the aid of references.

STANDARD: Identify deficiencies in regards to collective and individual training standards and resource allocations, providing recommendations for developing trainers, adjusting the training plan, correcting deficiencies, and conducting remedial training in accordance with MCO 1553.3A, Paragraph 6.e and MCRP 3-0A, Chapter 7.

PERFORMANCE STEPS:
1. Review the training and evaluation plan, T&R standards, MCCS, objectives, orders, METL, and doctrine.
2. Identify when the AAR will occur.
3. Select Potential AAR Sites
4. Choose training aids
5. Review the AAR Plan
6. Review training
7. Identify key events that observers/controllers are to observe
8. Collect observations from other observers/controllers
9. Organize observations (teaching points)
10. Reconnoiter the selected AAR site
11. Conduct rehearsal
12. Provide introduction and rules
13. Review training objectives
14. Review commander's mission and intent
15. Maintain focus on training objectives and established teaching points
16. Record key points and feedback
17. Identify tasks requiring re-training
18. Correct deficiencies i.e.: retrain immediately, revise SOPs, and integrate into future training plans

REFERENCES:
1. Army FM-101 Battle Focused Training (sept 90)
2. MCO 1553.3A Unit Training Management (UTM) (Jan 04)
3. MCRP 3-0A Unit Training Management Guide (Nov 96)
4. MCRP 3-0B How to Conduct Training (Nov 96)

URP-EVLI-2028: Evaluate Training

EVALUATION-CODED: NO   **SUSTAINMENT INTERVAL**: 24 months

DESCRIPTION: Utilizing performance checklists developed from collective or individual training events, observing performance of designated events, and providing written and oral feedback to the evaluated unit on proficiencies and deficiencies in relation to observed events.

GRADES: CPL, SGT, SSGT, GYSGT, 1STSGT, MSGT, MGYSGT, SGTMAJ, WO-1, CWO-2, CWO-3, CWO-4, CWO-5, 2NDLT, 1STLT, CAPT, MAJ, LTCOL

INITIAL TRAINING SETTING: FORMAL

CONDITION: Given a T&R Manual and with the aid of references.

STANDARD: To determine that training events are being executed to standard in accordance with MCO 1553.3A, Paragraph 6.e and MCRP 3-0A, chapter 7.

PERFORMANCE STEPS:
1. Develop Performance Evaluation checklists (PECL) based on collective/individual T&R Events.
2. Select Evaluators
3. Prepare Evaluators
4. Observe training
5. Document observed performance.
6. Analyze trends as a standard measuring tool to the evaluated unit.
7. Provide results to the evaluated unit.

REFERENCES:
1. Army FM-101 Battle Focused Training (Sep 90)
2. MCO 1553.3A Unit Training Management (UTM) (Jan 04)
3. MCRP 3-0A Unit Training Management Guide (Nov 96)

URP-IMPI-2024: Conduct Training

EVALUATION-CODED: NO   **SUSTAINMENT INTERVAL:** 24 months

DESCRIPTION: Training is performance-oriented and standards based.

GRADES: CPL, SGT, SSGT, GYSGT, 1STSGT, MSGT, MGYSGT, SGTMAJ, WO-1, CWO-2, CWO-3, CWO-4, CWO-5, 2NDLT, 1STLT, CAPT, MAJ, LTCOL, COL

INITIAL TRAINING SETTING: MOJT

CONDITION: Given a unit to train, approved Mission Essential Task List (METL), commander's training guidance, training plans, training schedules, trainers, T&R Manual, training resources, and with the aid of references.

STANDARD: So that all trainees meet or exceed the performance standards for each event and that all training complies with the intent of the training plan per the commander's guidance.

PERFORMANCE STEPS:
1. Review training materials.
2. Prepare for training.
3. Stage resources.
4. Account for personnel.
5. Conduct time critical Operational Risk Assessment (on-going).
6. Comply with installation and unit SOPs.
7. Conduct safety briefs, as required.
8. Execute planned training.
9. Supervise training.
10. Assess Operational Risk Management control measures.
11. Employ coaching.
12. Conduct immediate critique.

13. Conclude training.
14. Collect training data.
15. Account for personnel .
16. Account for resources.
17. Conduct training recovery.
18. Prepare for follow-on/remedial training.

REFERENCES:
1. Army FM-101 Battle Focused Training (Sep 90)
2. MCO 1553.3A Unit Training Management (UTM) (Jan 04)
3. MCO 3500.27B Operational Risk Management (ORM) (MAY 2004)
4. MCRP 3-0A Unit Training Management Guide (Nov 96)
5. MCRP 3-0B How to Conduct Training (Nov 96)

MISCELLANEOUS:

ADMINISTRATIVE INSTRUCTIONS: 1. Time Critical Operational Risk Assessment is conducted throughout training in a continuous cycle in order to address unexpected hazards that may arise. 2. The performance step "Collect training data," includes trainer observations, completion of performance checklists, completion of written tests (e.g. Marine Corps Common Skills) and other quantitative and qualitative data points, as required. 3. Support requirements are dictated by unit METL.

T3 T&R MANUAL

APPENDIX A

FUNCTIONAL AREA MATRIX

1000. FUNCTIONAL AREA MATRIX. The Functional Area Table includes the functional area description.

FUNCTIONAL AREA CODE	DESCRIPTION
AALT	Adult Learning Theory. A concept to consider throughout the SAT process. Adults are self-motivated. When developing, training and instruction consideration should be given to the knowledge and skills adults bring to the table acquired from personal experience.
ANLZ	Analyze. Job performance data is collected, analyzed, and reported. Perform job and task analysis, and develop instructional setting.
DESI	Design Instruction. Develop target population description, perform learning analysis (identify knowledge/skills required for T&R's developed in analyze phase) and develop Terminal Learning Objectives.
DEVI	Develop Instruction. Develop course structure, concept cards, and then conduct ORAW. Develop lesson materials, construct tests, and validate instruction. Finally, develop CDD and POI. This phase represents the bulk of the training materials and documents.
IMPI	Implement Instruction. During this phase, lesson materials are reviewed, and instructor will prepare for and conduct instruction. (Time critical ORA happens here) Instructor will also administer student tests and perform After Lesson Management.
EVLI	Evaluate Instruction. This phase applies to all other phases, and is performed continuously. A plan for validation should be made, identifying the best evaluation approach for the training. Any evaluation issues are identified. The evaluation method selected is employed, data is collected and analyzed, and finally, data is interpreted to develop a plan to improve training.
MANI	Manage Instruction. Includes such skills as using MCTIMS to register and track training, performing self-inspections of the unit training, staff and faculty development, certifications, and the like.
TIMS	Training Information Management System. All tasks relating to the use of the Marine Corps Training Information Management System (MCTIMS) for the recording of learning analysis, learning objectives, concept cards, course descriptive data and program of instruction data.

T3 T&R MANUAL

APPENDIX B

TERMS AND DEFINITIONS

Terms in this glossary are subject to change as applicable orders and directives are revised. Terms established by Marine Corps orders or directives take precedence after definitions found in Joint Pub 1-02, *DOD Dictionary of Military and Associated Terms.*

A

After Action Review. A professional discussion of training events conducted after all training to promote learning among training participants. The formality and scope increase with the command level and size of the training evolution. For longer exercises, they should be planned for at predetermined times during an exercise. The results of the AAR shall be recorded on an after action report and forwarded to higher headquarters. The commander and higher headquarters use the results of an AAR to reallocate resources, reprioritize their training plan, and plan for future training.

Assessment. An informal judgment of the unit's proficiency and resources made by a commander or trainer to gain insight into the unit's overall condition. It serves as the basis for the midrange plan. Commanders make frequent use of these determinations during the course of the combat readiness cycle in order to adjust, prioritize or modify training events and plans.

C

Chaining. A process that enables unit leaders to effectively identify subordinate's collective events and individual events that support a specific collective event. For example, collective training events at the 4000-level are directly supported by collective events at the 3000-level. Utilizing the building block approach to progressive training, these collective events are further supported by individual training events at the 1000 and 2000-levels. When a higher-level event by its nature requires the completion of lower level events, they are "chained"; Sustainment credit is given for all lower level events chained to a higher event.

Collective Event. A clearly defined, discrete, and measurable activity, action, or event (i.e., task) that requires organized team or unit performance and leads to accomplishment of a mission or function. A collective task is derived from unit missions or higher-level collective tasks. Task accomplishment requires performance of procedures composed of supporting collective or individual tasks. A collective task describes the exact performance a group must perform in the field under actual operational conditions. The term "collective" does not necessarily infer that a unit accomplishes the event. A unit, such as a squad or platoon conducting an attack; may accomplish a collective event or, it may be accomplished by an individual to accomplish a unit mission, such as a battalion supply officer completing a reconciliation of the battalion's CMR. Thus, many collective events will have titles that are the same as individual events; however, the standard and condition will be different because the scope of the collective event is broader.

Collective Training Standards (CTS). Criteria that specify mission and functional area unit proficiency standards for combat, combat support, and combat service support units. They include tasks, conditions, standards, evaluator instruction, and key indicators. CTS are found within collective training events in T&R Manuals.

Combat Readiness Cycle. The combat readiness cycle depicts the relationships within the building block approach to training. The combat readiness cycle progresses from T&R Manual individual core skills training, to the accomplishment of collective training events, and finally, to a unit's participation in a contingency or actual combat. The combat readiness cycle demonstrates the relationship of core capabilities to unit combat readiness. Individual core skills training and the training of collective events lead to unit proficiency and the ability to accomplish the unit's stated mission.

Combat Readiness Percentage (CRP). The CRP is a quantitative numerical value used in calculating collective training readiness based on the E-coded events that support the unit METL. CRP is a concise measure of unit training accomplishments. This numerical value is only a snapshot of training readiness at a specific time. As training is conducted, unit CRP will continuously change.

Component Events. Component events are the major tasks involved in accomplishing a collective event. Listing these tasks guide Marines toward the accomplishment of the event and help evaluators determine if the task has been done to standard. These events may be lower-level collective or individual events that must be accomplished.

Condition. The condition describes the training situation or environment under which the training event or task will take place. Expands on the information in the title by identifying when, where and why the event or task will occur and what materials, personnel, equipment, environmental provisions, and safety constraints must be present to perform the event or task in a real-world environment. Commanders can modify the conditions of the event to best prepare their Marines to accomplish the assigned mission (e.g. in a desert environment; in a mountain environment; etc.).

Core Competency. Core competency is the comprehensive measure of a unit's ability to accomplish its assigned MET. It serves as the foundation of the T&R Program. Core competencies are those unit core capabilities and individual core skills that support the commander's METL and T/O mission statement. Individual competency is exhibited through demonstration of proficiency in specified core tasks and core plus tasks. Unit proficiency is measured through collective tasks.

Core Capabilities. Core capabilities are the essential functions a unit must be capable of performing during extended contingency/combat operations. Core unit capabilities are based upon mission essential tasks derived from operational plans; doctrine and established tactics; techniques and procedures.

Core Plus Capabilities. Core plus capabilities are advanced capabilities that are environment, mission, or theater specific. Core plus capabilities may entail high-risk, high-cost training for missions that are less likely to be assigned in combat.

Core Plus Skills. Core plus skills are those advanced skills that are environment, mission, rank, or billet specific. 2000-level training is designed to make Marines proficient in core skills in a specific billet or at a specified rank at the Combat Ready level. 3000-8000-level training produces combat leaders and fully qualified section members at the Combat Qualified level. Marines trained at the Combat Qualified level are those the commanding officer feels are capable of accomplishing unit-level missions and of directing the actions of subordinates. Many core plus tasks are learned via MOJT, while others form the base for curriculum in career level MOS courses taught by the formal school.

Core Skills. Core skills are those essential basic skills that "make" a Marine and qualify that Marine for an MOS. They are the 1000-level skills introduced in entry-level training at formal schools and refined in operational units.

D

Defense Readiness Reporting System (DRRS). A comprehensive readiness reporting system that evaluates readiness on the basis of the actual missions and capabilities assigned to the forces. It is a capabilities-based, adaptive, near real-time reporting system for the entire Department of Defense.

Deferred Event. A T&R event that a commanding officer may postpone when in his or her judgment, a lack of logistic support, ammo, ranges, or other training assets requires a temporary exemption. CRP cannot be accrued for deferred "E-Coded" events.

Delinquent Event. An event becomes delinquent when a Marine or unit exceeds the sustainment interval for that particular event. The individual or unit must update the delinquent event by first performing all prerequisite events. When the unit commander deems that performing all prerequisite is unattainable, then the delinquent event will be re-demonstrated under the supervision of the appropriate evaluation authority.

E

E-Coded Event. An "E-Coded" event is a collective T&R event that is a noted indicator of capability or, a noted Collective skill that contributes to the unit's ability to perform the supported MET. As such, only "E-Coded" events are assigned a CRP value and used to calculate a unit's CRP.

Entry-level training. Pipeline training that equips students for service with the Marine Operating Forces.

Evaluation. Evaluation is a continuous process that occurs at all echelons, during every phase of training and can be both formal and informal. Evaluations ensure that Marines and units are capable of conducting their combat mission. Evaluation results are used to reallocate resources, reprioritize the training plan, and plan for future training.

Event (Training). 1) An event is a significant training occurrence that is identified, expanded and used as a building block and potential milestone for a unit's training. An event may include formal evaluations. 2) An event within the T&R Program can be an individual training evolution, a collective training evolution or both. Through T&R events, the unit commander ensures that individual Marines and the unit progress from a combat capable status to a Fully Combat Qualified (FCQ) status.

Event Component. The major procedures (i.e., actions) that must occur to perform a Collective Event to standard.

Exercise Commander (EC). The Commanding General, Marine Expeditionary Force or his appointee will fill this role, unless authority is delegated to the respective commander of the Division, Wing, or FSSG. Responsibilities and functions of the EC include: 1) designate unit(s) to be evaluated, 2) may designate an exercise director, 3) prescribe exercise objectives and T&R events to be evaluated, 4) coordinate with commands or agencies external to the Marine Corps and adjacent Marine Corps commands, when required.

Exercise Director (ED). Designated by the EC to prepare, conduct, and report all evaluation results. Responsibilities and functions of the ED include: 1) Publish a letter of instruction (LOI) that: delineates the T&R events to be evaluated, establishes timeframe of the exercise, lists responsibilities of various elements participating in the exercise, establishes safety requirements/guidelines, and lists coordinating instructions. 2) Designate the TEC and TECG to operate as the central control agency for the exercise. 3) Assign evaluators, to include the senior evaluator, and ensure that those evaluators are properly trained. 4) Develop the general exercise scenario taking into account any objectives/events prescribed by the EC. 5) Arrange for all resources to include: training areas, airspace, aggressor forces, and other required support.

I

Individual Readiness. The individual training readiness of each Marine is measured by the number of individual events required and completed for the rank or billet currently held.

Individual Training. Training that applies to individual Marines. Examples include rifle qualifications and HMMWV driver licensing.

Individual Training Standards (ITS). Specifies training tasks and standards for each MOS or specialty within the Marine Corps. In most cases, once an MOS or community develops a T&R, the ITS order will be cancelled. However, most communities will probably fold a large portion of their ITS into their new T&R manual.

M

Marine Corps Combat Readiness and Evaluation System (MCCRES). An evaluation system designed to provide commanders with a comprehensive set of mission performance standards from which training programs can be developed; and through which the efficiency and effectiveness of training can be evaluated. The Ground T&R Program will eventually replace MCCRES.

Marine Corps Ground Training and Readiness (T&R) Program. The T&R Program is the Marine Corps' primary tool for planning and conducting training, for planning and conducting training evaluation, and for assessing training readiness. The program will provide the commander with standardized programs of instruction for units within the ground combat, combat support, and combat service support communities. It consolidates the ITS, CTS, METL and other individual and unit training management tools. T&R is a program of standards that systematizes commonly accepted skills, is open to innovative change, and above all, tailors the training effort to the unit's mission. Further, T&R serves as a training guide and provides commanders an immediate assessment of unit combat readiness by assigning a CRP to key training events. In short, the T&R Program is a building block approach to training that maximizes flexibility and produces the best-trained Marines possible.

Mission Essential Task(s) MET(s). A MET is a collective task in which an organization must be proficient in order to accomplish an appropriate portion of its wartime mission(s). MET listings are the foundation for the T&R manual; all events in the T&R manual support a MET.

Mission Essential Task List (METL). Descriptive training document that provides units a clear, war fighting focused description of collective actions necessary to achieve wartime mission proficiency. The service-level METL, that which is used as the foundation of the T&R manual, is developed using Marine Corps doctrine, operational plans, T/Os, UJTL, UNTL, and MCTL. For community based T&R manuals, an occupational field METL is developed to focus the community's collective training standards. Commanders develop their unit METL from the service-level METL, operational plans, contingency plans, and SOPs.

Mission Performance Standards (MPS). Criteria that specify mission and functional area unit proficiency standards for combat, combat support and combat service support units. They include tasks, conditions, standards, evaluator instruction, and key indicators. MPS are contained within the MCCRES volumes. The MCCRES volumes are being replaced by T&R Manuals. Collective events will replace MPS.

O

Operational Readiness (DOD, NATO). OR is the capability of a unit/formation, ship, weapon system, or equipment to perform the missions or functions for which it is organized or designed. May be used in a general sense or to express a level or degree of readiness.

P

Performance Step. Performance steps are included in the components of an Individual T&R Event. They are the major procedures (i.e., actions) a unit Marine must accomplish to perform an individual event to standard. They describe the procedure the task performer must take to perform the task under operational conditions and provide sufficient information for a task performer to perform the procedure (may necessitate identification of supporting steps, procedures, or actions in outline form). Performance steps follow a logical progression and should be followed sequentially, unless otherwise stated. Normally, performance steps are listed only for 1000-level individual events (those that are taught in the entry-level MOS school). Listing performance steps is optional if the steps are already specified in a published reference.

Prerequisite Event. Prerequisites are the academic training and/or T&R events that must be completed prior to attempting the event.

R

Readiness (DOD). Readiness is the ability of U.S. military forces to fight and meet the demands of the national military strategy. Readiness is the synthesis of two distinct but interrelated levels: a) Unit readiness--The ability to provide capabilities required by combatant commanders to execute assigned missions. This is derived from the ability of each unit to deliver the outputs for which it was designed. b) Joint readiness--The combatant commander's ability to integrate and synchronize ready combat and support forces to execute assigned missions.

S

Section Skill Tasks. Section skills are those competencies directly related to unit functioning. They are group rather than individual in nature, and require participation by a section (S-1, S-2, S-3, etc).

Simulation Training. Simulators provide the additional capability to develop and hone core and core plus skills. Accordingly, the development of simulator training events for appropriate T&R syllabi can help maintain valuable combat resources while reducing training time and cost. Therefore, in cases where simulator fidelity and capabilities are such that simulator training closely matches that of actual training events, T&R Manual developers may include the option of using simulators to accomplish the training. CRP credit will be earned for E-coded simulator events based on assessment of relative training event performance.

Standard. A standard is a statement that establishes criteria for how well a task or learning objective must be performed. The standard specifies how well, completely, or accurately a process must be performed or product produced. For higher-level collective events, it describes why the event is being done and the desired end-state of the event. Standards become more specific for lower-level events and outline the accuracy, time limits, sequencing, quality, product, process, restrictions, etc., that indicate the minimum acceptable level of performance required of the event. At a minimum, both collective and individual training standards consist of a task, the condition under which the task is to be performed, and the evaluation criteria that will be used to verify that the task has been performed to a satisfactory level.

Sustainment Training. Periodic retraining or demonstration of an event required maintaining the minimum acceptable level of proficiency or capability required to accomplish a training objective. Sustainment training goes beyond the entry-level and is designed to maintain or further develop proficiency in a given set of skills.

B-6

Systems Approach to Training (SAT). An orderly process for analyzing, designing, developing, implementing, and evaluating a unit's training program to ensure the unit, and the Marines of that unit acquire the knowledge and skills essential for the successful conduct of the unit's wartime missions.

T

Training Task. This describes a direct training activity that pertains to an individual Marine. A task is composed of 3 major components: a description of what is to be done, a condition, and a standard.

Technical Exercise Controller (TEC). The TEC is appointed by the ED, and usually comes from his staff or a subordinate command. The TEC is the senior evaluator within the TECG and should be of equal or higher grade than the commander(s) of the unit(s) being evaluated. The TEC is responsible for ensuring that the evaluation is conducted following the instructions contained in this order and MCO 1553.3A. Specific T&R manuals are used as the source for evaluation criteria.

Tactical Exercise Control Group (TECG). A TECG is formed to provide subject matter experts in the functional areas being evaluated. The benefit of establishing a permanent TECG is to have resident, dedicated evaluation authority experience, and knowledgeable in evaluation technique. The responsibilities and functions of the TECG include: 1) developing a detailed exercise scenario to include the objectives and events prescribed by the EC/ED in the exercise LOI; 2) conducting detailed evaluator training prior to the exercise; 3) coordinating and controlling role players and aggressors; 4) compiling the evaluation data submitted by the evaluators and submitting required results to the ED; 5) preparing and conducting a detailed exercise debrief for the evaluated unit(s).

Training Plan. A training plan is a document that outlines the general plan for the conduct of individual and collective training in an organization for specified periods of time.

U

Unit CRP. Unit CRP is a percentage of the E-coded collective events that support the unit METL accomplished by the unit. Unit CRP is the average of all MET CRP.

Unit Evaluation. All units in the Marine Corps must be evaluated, either formally or informally, to ensure they are capable of conducting their combat mission. Informal evaluations should take place during all training events. The timing of formal evaluations is critical and should, when appropriate, be directly related to the units' operational deployment cycle. Formal evaluations should take place after the unit has been staffed with the majority of its personnel, has had sufficient time to train to individual and collective standards, and early enough in the training cycle so there is sufficient time to correctly identified weaknesses prior to deployment. All combat units and units' task organized for combat require formal evaluations prior to operational deployments.

Unit Training Management (UTM). Unit training management is the use of the SAT and Marine Corps training principles in a manner that maximizes training results and focuses the training priorities of the unit on its wartime mission. UTM governs the major peacetime training activity of the Marine Corps and applies to all echelons of the Total Force.

W

Waived Event. An event that is waived by a commanding officer when in his or her judgment, previous experience or related performance satisfies the requirement of a particular event.